FORTY SHADES OF GREEN

Short Stories by Writers
From Northern Ireland

Edited by

SUZI BLAIR

NEW FICTION

First published in 1993 by
NEW FICTION
4 Hythegate, Werrington
Peterborough,
PE4 7ZP

Printed in Great Britain by Forward Press.

Foreword

The advent of New Fiction signifies the expansion of what has traditionally been, a limited platform for writers of short stories. New Fiction aims to promote new short stories to the widest possible audience.

New Fiction collections represent the wealth of new talent in writing, and provide enjoyable, interesting and readable stories appealing to a diversity of tastes.

Intriguing and entertaining; from sharp character sketches to 'slice of life' situations, the stories have been selected because each one is *a good read*.

This collection of short stories is from the pens of the people of Northern Ireland. They are new stories, sweeping across the spectrums of style and subject to reflect the richness of character intrinsic to the region, today.

Suzi Blair
Editor.

Contents

Ballyrowan in Winter

by

Violet Surgenor

In the small town of Ballyrowan, right up in the north of Ireland, people were glad to be settling down again after the hustle and bustle of the busy summer season. As Ballyrowan ground to a halt, down came the gaily coloured bunting and the bright fairy lights. Flower beds that had spelled out the town's name in a variety of colours were dug over and fed with fertilizer and left brown and dull until the following spring. Buckets and spades, beach balls and plastic windmills were stored away by shopkeepers as they prepared for the slower pace of the winter trade. Now was the time to relax and put one's feet up, for in winter, Ballyrowan was a quiet sleepy town where nothing ever happened. Well, where usually, nothing ever happened.

But in number six, Seaview Terrace, a row of twelve cottages facing out over the small harbour, Ted Riley was staring open mouthed at his wife, Maisie. The veins on his neck stood out in vivid purple lines, his face was suffused with red blotches and small specks of spittle were escaping from his mouth.

Barely able to control himself he roared, 'She's what? Are you sure? Where is she? I'll shake the living daylights out of her. Where is she?'

'Now Ted, calm down. There's no good in you losing your temper. That won't help matters.' Maisie held up her hand as if to hold him at bay.

Roughly he pushed his way past her into the hall and, taking the stairs three at a time, he burst into his daughter's bedroom. 'Joanie. Is this true? Is this right what your mother has been telling me?' he yelled at her.

Joanie, her face pale with fright, lay in bed clutching the bedclothes tightly around her. She glanced fearfully at her mother, who had come into the room behind her father. She nodded her head and stared numbly at the bedspread she was twisting between her trembling fingers.

'Who was it? Who is responsible? I'll break his neck. I'll kill him.' Ted Riley bellowed like a maddened bull.

Her voice shaking with fear, Joanie whispered, 'I don't know who it was.'

Her father's face suddenly went slack, his mouth hung open and saliva trickled down his chin. His voice hoarse with emotion he said, 'You don't know who it was? Dear God, I'm a councillor. I am a respected member of this town's

1

council and my daughter is pregnant and doesn't know who is responsible. How many were there, for God's sake?' His voice rose now like a roar of thunder as he reached out for her.

'My God, will you listen to that.' Next door in number eight, Maggie Craig was serving up dinner to her husband, Tom, and their two young children. She nodded towards the Riley's house. 'Did you ever hear the like of it?'

Tom shook his head and half heartedly began to eat. His face was more lined than usual and his eyes were ringed with dark shadows.

'I wonder what on earth is going on in there?' asked Maggie. 'Councillor Riley seems to be having problems.' There was a sneer in her voice.

'How would I know? Anyway I'm not interested in them in there.' Tom Craig snapped at his wife. He was more concerned about the auditors who were at this moment going through the books in the furniture shop he worked in. His stomach churned as he nervously ran his fingers through his thin dark hair. Would they spot the receipts he had altered, he wondered anxiously? He never would have done it except he was so desperate. Mickey Dooney, at the bookies was threatening him and where else could he lay his hands on five hundred pounds? He could feel the sweat in his armpits as he thought of what could happen to him if the auditors noticed the alterations on the receipt copies. But maybe they wouldn't notice. If they didn't see the slight changes in the figures, he would be in the clear. That was his only hope. Tom Craig prayed as he had never prayed in his life before.

Down in number four, Seaview Terrace, Edna Wilson closed her mind to the yelling and shouting going on in number six. She had never had a high opinion of Ted Riley or that daughter of his. She wore far too much make-up and her skirt was so short it just wasn't decent.

Edna was quietly reading again the letter that had arrived that morning. It was from her only son, James, who lived in Melbourne in Australia. It was nearly twelve years since she had encouraged him to emigrate, although it had nearly broken her heart. But what future was there for a bright go-ahead young lad like James in a small seaside resort like Ballyrowan? She had practically forced him to go. Told him she would be perfectly alright on her own. She had plenty of friends and wouldn't be lonely. So he had left Ballyrowan and his mother, and Dear Lord, how she missed him. She lived for his letters. She scoured them eagerly for every scrap of news. She had cried bitterly when he got married. She would have given anything to have been with him, to meet

Alison, her future daughter-in-law, and just to be near them. But James was still struggling to set up his own business and neither of them had the money for the fare to Australia. Somehow the years had rolled by and still she had never managed to visit them. Now she had two grandchildren that she had never seen except in photographs. Jimmy, who was almost ten, and so like his father, with the same determined smile and same unruly brown hair. And Sarah, only six and the picture of her mother, Alison; tall and fair with wide blue eyes.

With a sigh Edna dropped the letter onto her lap. James and Alison had invited her to come and visit them for Christmas, which was a lovely idea and oh, how she would dearly love to go, but where was the money to come from? James hadn't mentioned the fare so perhaps he assumed she was able to afford it. But Edna lived on only a small pension which did not allow her any spare cash for luxuries or indeed any savings. She had always to scrimp and save to be able to send out presents for birthdays and Christmas.

Well, she would just have to refuse their invitation. She could not afford the fare and nothing would make her ask her son for money. Oh, she knew she was being foolish, but her pride would not allow her to ask. She would write and tell them she had other plans for Christmas. It was unfortunate, but there it was. Edna stood up and went over to the window to look out at the harbour. It was a fine evening and with dusk falling the small boats appeared as dark shadows looming on the water. Leaning against the harbour wall was Tom Craig, his hands thrust deep into his pockets and his shoulders hunched as he stared moodily at the water. He looked so worried and dejected that Edna was about to go out and ask what was wrong, when abruptly he turned and walked across the narrow street and went into his house. Edna shook her head sadly. It looked as if she wasn't the only person in Ballyrowan that night with things on her mind. She decided to have an early night. Maybe after a good nights sleep she would be able to come up with some believable reasons for not wanting to visit her son and his family for the first time in twelve years.

Arthur Mitchell was able to tell everyone about the goings on in Seaview Terrace the next morning. Hadn't he just been dandering along as usual with his postbag over his shoulder and a handful of letters ready to be shoved through the various letterboxes, when he noticed Sergeant Telford's police car parked outside number eight. That was where Tom Craig and his family lived. But that's not all. Just as he reached number six, the door opened and who should come out but young Joanie Riley with her face all puffy and blotched as if she had just spent half the night crying her eyes out. And what's more, she was carrying a great big suitcase, and without even a glance in his direction, she headed down the street and never once looked back. And as he watched Joanie disappearing around the corner, Arthur heard the sound of another door opening and turned round to see Sergeant Telford emerging from Tom Craig's house and holding onto Tom's arm as if he was afraid Tom was going to run away. Arthur was also able to divulge that Mr Taylor, who owned the furniture shop, was there also, with his face down to his knees and poor Maggie Craig standing in the doorway wringing her hands and begging Mr Taylor to have mercy. But the three men ignored her pleas and got into the police car and drove off.

But to Arthur's mind, the strangest thing of all was what happened next. Edna Wilson had come out of number four to see what was going on and Arthur handed her a letter which was her second one from Australia in two days. Well, everyone knew how Edna looked forward to getting those letters from that son of hers. She tore the envelope open right there on the doorstep and something fell out. Arthur thought it looked like some kind of travel ticket. Edna then gave what Arthur could only describe as a squeal of delight, flung her arms around his neck and gave him a great wet kiss on the cheek. Prim Edna Wilson who would hardly pass the time of day with you. Arthur hadn't got over the shock yet.

As things settled down again in Ballyrowan, there were those who said wasn't it a great shame about Joanie Riley. But then, you couldn't really expect anything else from a girl like that. There were one or two others who were very relieved to see her going and hoped never to hear from her.

Everyone was shocked when they heard about Tom Craig. Mr Taylor's business boomed for a couple of weeks as people flocked to the shop to hear, in confidence of course, all the details of Tom Craig's means of supporting his gambling habits. Who really knew just how much Tom had stolen from him, Mr Taylor would say with a suggestive shrug of his shoulders.

Edna Wilson flew off to Australia, and wasn't it lovely to see her so happy and smiling. They wouldn't be surprised if she stayed there with her son and his family. After all, hadn't she been talking about it for years?

After all the excitement things seemed very dull in Ballyrowan. It was a cold wet winter and a fierce wind blew in from the Atlantic making everyone shiver and wish heartily that summer was here. At least then it wouldn't be so dull.

The Mission

by

John McDowell

It was 1973. Belfast was a very different city then. It didn't appear so to many
of its inhabitants but the city was at the nadir of its fortunes. 'Polarisation' as
the politicians had begun to call it was at its most arctic extreme. The consequences of the protagonists gambits - Bloody Sunday, The Abercorn, Oxford
Street - were fresh in the air. 'The nearer the source, the clearer the stream', and
religious hatred had never been more crystal clear. As Michael sat on the
number thirty-three bus he too was unaware of the horrifying depths to which
the morals and morale of his countrymen had sunk. He was feeling most con-
tent.

He amused himself by thinking what his fellow travellers would feel had they
been aware of the purpose of his mission. He knew the answer. Each would
have been utterly sickened. But Michael knew his own mind. He was seventeen
and intelligent; very intelligent indeed, some of his teachers had said at the
grammar school. This thought was constantly in his mind and as though to cor-
roborate it he recited to himself some lines from Pope
> 'So clocks to lead their nimble motions owe,
> The Springs above urged by the weight below;
> The ponderous Ballance keeps its poise the same,
> Actuates, Maintains, and rules the moving frame.'

Today he felt purposeful and adult. He felt self-sufficient in a way he had
never felt before, and although he did not know it, he would never feel again.
Today was the culmination of eighteen months of thought and preparation. He
had begun by writing to England. Month by month the plain buff envelopes had
arrived and Michael had built up a sound knowledge of the principles involved
and felt able to defend them in argument. He had practised at home with his
mother and father but they had been reduced to incoherent rage after the open
sallies. Nevertheless he thought he would make a good apologist in any company. He was much less sure of the practical issues, but he knew that better
men than he had lived by them, and today's mission was the first step towards
putting the theory into practise.

5

He alighted from the bus at Wellington Place taking care not to bang the plastic bag which had been resting at his feet. The first thing he noticed was the burnt out shell of a lately bombed restaurant. He walked over to the building to take a closer look. Another older man was standing in what, until the previous night, had been the entrance way to the building. 'Probably a policeman' Michael thought.

'Any casualties.'

'No - thanks be to God.'

'Good' Michael thought. He lit a cigarette.

He walked down to Donegall Place and stood for a minute looking across at the City Hall, a mock Palladian building considerably out of proportion with the rest of the buildings in the Square. Michael thought of the councillors and local government officials within. He remembered a story told to him by his politics teacher at school about Belfast Corporation in the 1930's. A Unionist Alderman had been inveighing against the high rate of inflation and describing how it would reduce the councils ability to build new houses and repair old ones, particularly in the west of the city. At the end of the speech one of his colleagues had stood up to support the mayor's prudence. His words were to the effect that all reasonable men were aware of the difficulties which the Corporation faced in administering its processes especially at this time when inflation, like a giant octopus, was spreading its testicles all over Northern Ireland. For Michael the story summed up the crassness and boorishness of Unionism. A creed which was supposed to be his heritage.

As he turned sharply to go he collided with two nuns who had been queuing behind him to cross the road. The bag he was carrying dropped from his hand and fell to the ground. Unknown to him, the minute hand of the clock inside broke off.

'Shit! - sorry sister.'

He picked the bag up and walked on. He glanced at his watch - '11.30 am - time for a pint.'

He knew many of the bars in town and liked most of them. There was nothing quite like the atmosphere in a Belfast pub, and nothing in Belfast pubs was quite like the atmosphere in McGlades. He headed off towards the far end of Royal Avenue and within ten minutes was sitting on a high stool in the upstairs lounge contemplating a pint of Harp. He had first drunk in town when he was just sixteen when the fashion for long hair and heavy side-boards had made the discernment of age almost impossible for publicans. He had come to know Siobhan, the barmaid at McGlades, quite well. She came from Divis street in

6

the lower Falls and Michael was fairly certain that she knew him to be under age but ignored it. He knew that she liked him. One day when he had been sitting alone reading a book on Irish History she had come over and sat beside him during her lunch hour. Seeing the book she assumed he was a Catholic and had told him stories about her brothers ordeals in 'Long Kesh' the prison outside Belfast. That's what Michael liked about Irish Catholics. They were a community, one faith, one nation - a freemasonry of sanctified adversity.

Unfortunately Siobhan wasn't on today and the barman, the proprietor's son was chatting to some journalists at the far end of the bar. Michael reached down into the bag and groping carefully among the contents took out a book and began to read. It was 'The Great Hunger', Cecil Woodham Smith's account of the condition of Ireland during the years of the Famine. He read intently, occasionally marking important passages. More often than not they were quotations from the letters of Charles Edward Trevelyan, Assistant Secretary to the Treasury, Clapham seat philanthropist and incorruptible zealot for the improvement of public administration.

In October 1846 during the second year of the famine when the potato crop had failed completely he had written 'all we can safely aim at is to accomplish such a just distribution and equalisation of the existing stock of food that the people in every part of Ireland may have the opportunity of purchasing food at current prices, if they have the means to do so.'

Those who had not the means to buy 'must be placed on a charitable footing.' Michael thought that this statement would look ordinary, even benign, out of its historical context. However on the following page he read the report of a post-mortem on a man engaged in a poor relief scheme of road-building. 'There was no food whatever in Dennis Kennedy's small intestine, but in the large intestine was 'a portion of undigested raw cabbage, mixed with excrement'.

When Michael left the bar at about 1.30 his mind was suffused with the vicarious indignation which is the prerogative of the remotest onlooker to a distant tragedy.

He walked down Donegall Street and on to High Street, turning right into Church Lane. He pushed open a glass door and walked up to the counter.

'McWilliams. I've an appointment for 1.30.'

'Ok. You're a bit late - You can go over to the basin now. Shelly, your 1.30's here now - Can I take your coat and bag.'

Michael took his coat off. 'I'll just hold onto the bag if you don't mind.'

He sat down in the chair and placed his neck in the cleft made by the v shaped protrusion of the hairdresser's wash basin, and contemplated a large

7

damp spot on the ceiling. Twenty seconds later he was peering at the face of the assistant.

'Water all right for you?'

'Yes, fine thanks.'

Michael enjoyed having his hair washed and involuntarily closed his eyes to savour the experience. As the girl was working in the second shampoo he thought he could hear her whispering about him to her colleague and imagined her glancing at his relaxed face, fancying him.

When she had finished he got up to take his seat in front of a mirror. As he passed out of earshot the assistant said to her friend, 'I hate it when they come in stinking of drink.'

As usual the haircut was not what Michael had hoped it would be. He had a double crown and his hair sat up like a semi-beehive on the side opposite the parting. He thought that it destroyed the symmetry of his face and looked a little effeminate.

'How's that' will that do?'

'Yes, fine.' He tipped the receptionist on the way out. He had one more call to make before he could set about the proper purpose of his journey. On his way back through town he stopped to look in the window of Burton's 'The fifty shilling tailor' his father called them. He had been trying to encourage Michael to buy a suit or rather to have one bought for him. The shop was full of people who looked just like his father. But for the measuring tapes that hung like clergyman's stoles around their necks it would have been impossible to tell the managers from the customers. The sight caused Michael to wonder what his father would say if he knew, or rather when he found out, what Michael was doing. He had had the same thoughts, a hundred, a thousand times before. He rehearsed the arguments again. It was his life; he was an independent human being and must be led by his own lights. A lot of other intelligent people had done it. It was something which he felt he must do, and today he was going to strike the first blow for his freedom. But behind all the arguments he knew the anguish and shame he would cause. He moved on. Just one more call.

He walked back into Donegall Place. The city was not as busy as it had been. People were afraid to come out at night because of the bombs, but the shops and bars were doing good trade that Saturday afternoon. It always amazed Michael how much people smiled as they walked and chatted through town. He was used to coming in alone, drinking and reading. He was not resentful of them but his earlier contentment had faded and he was feeling irritable. Perhaps it was the hair cuttings lodged in his shirt.

8

He walked towards Castle Junction and cut into a narrow street, almost an alleyway. He approached a building which looked derelict, he pushed open the heavy metal door and began to climb the five flights of stairs which led him to the workshop at the top. He tried the handle but the door was locked as he had known it would be. First removing his book, he set the bag down carefully beside the doorway, turned and descended the stairs.

It was raining now and Michael walked swiftly towards St Mary's Church, blessing himself as he passed by. He opened the door of the little repository opposite and stepped inside. He walked up to the counter and pointing high to the right hand side of the display window said, 'I would like that Crucifix please - the large dark brown one for £7.99.'

The shop assistant, an elderly shabbily dressed man picked up a bamboo cane, took aim, flicked the bottom of the crucifix with the cane and caught it just before it hit a little delft Madonna and Child. He wrapped it in brown paper and gave it to Michael.

The anxieties which had begun to afflict him became worse as Michael got on the bus to go home. He felt sure that people were glaring at the oddly shaped parcel which was swinging casually in his right hand. His anxiety worsened as he thought about what his father would say when he got home. Anxiety became panic when a man he knew sat down beside him for several stops.

'What's in the parcel?'

'An aeroplane.'

'Are you not a bit old for that?'

'No it's one of those remote controlled ones. I'm in the club at school.'

The man looked pityingly at Michael for a moment.

'What's that then?'

The head of Christ with an unusually sharp crown of thorns had torn through the brown paper package.

'I don't know, I haven't looked at it properly yet - my stop, excuse me.'

Michael walked slowly home. He opened the door and shouted. There was nobody there. He unwrapped the crucifix and tried it in various positions on his bedroom wall. It looked best in the place where the block mounting of Picasso's Blue Nude usually hung. He was fed up with that anyway. He opened his wardrobe and put the offending masterpiece behind a pile of shoe boxes. He half closed the wardrobe door but opened it again, kneeling down to pull out the bottom most box. He opened it and removed twelve buff coloured envelopes. He took out the contents of the first envelope. It was a letter marked

9

'Catholic Enquiry Centre, 120 Westheath Road, London, WN3 7TY'. Attached to it was a small pamphlet - No. 44. 'The Catholic Church'. He glanced at the contents, put it back in the envelope and replaced the shoe box. He returned to the crucifix. He had just hammered in a nail when he heard the door open and his mother and father come in.

'Hello, Hello, Michael are you home son?'

He heard his fathers steps begin to climb the stairs.

'Did you leave your granny's clock into your Uncle Albert's to get fixed?'

'Yes; he wasn't in so I left it at the workshop door like you told me.'

'Good lad.'

He could just see his fathers hand as it rested on the top of the bannister.

'Hey dad, you'll never guess what I've bought.'

Goldilocks

by

Rose Gallacher

Goldilocks was taking a long leisurely walk in the woods. Not by choice, mind you. That morning her mother had opened the front door, took her by the arm, deposited her on the front step and said, 'Get lost you little toe-rag.'

She slouched along, hands deep in her pockets, muttering to herself. The sun was shining through the trees, and the little woodland birds were twittering, and flitting from bush to bush.

'Silly chirping buggers,' Goldilocks thought. 'I wish I had my slingshot.'

Goldilocks as you can gather was not a happy child. No indeed. She came into the world on *that* auspicious day, bawling discontentedly. And it seemed she would leave the *said* world bawling discontentedly, with barely a break in between.

At the moment it was her hair. How she loathed that long curly yellow mane, that stopped half an inch above her bum. It was indeed a handicap. The source of many disappointments. Why only yesterday the skinhead brigade, who smoked and planned behind the bike sheds at school, told her to 'go play with her dolls', when she expressed a wish to join the gang. They also lobbed a few stones after her.

Now at this point in time, let us move from the discontented Goldilocks, and meet the other characters in our story. The bear family. Mr James Bear, Miz Imelda Bear and young Vinney.

The Bears owned a little property in the woods, nothing flash, just a little one up, one down, but in very good condition. The Bears were also strolling the woods that morning, chatting and taking in the sights. As a family, they were quite health conscious. Deep abdominal breathings, long walks and quick jogs, were the norm for them before high fibre breakfasts.

Now the rest of the story you know, how Goldilocks ate the porridge, broke the chair, and lay on the clean duvet with her shoes on. But perhaps you don't know that Goldilocks never returned home - Never Ever - much to the relief of her long suffering mother.

I think myself, that the Bear family, being a socially minded responsible group, had long conversations with her, and as a result decided to adopt her. *Or*

11

perhaps she fell prey to one of Mr Bears peculiar little quirks. You see James Bear was at that very annoying age, known as the 'Male Menopausal Syndrome' in some circles. Sometimes he couldn't stop himself staring at young girl's legs, and other growing parts. Maybe he, much to the consternation of himself and Miz Imelda, set Goldilocks up in a little hut, four trees away, as his 'mistress'.

Or again perhaps, they all just ate her.

The Belfast Leprechauns

by

Seamus Sheridan

Ireland is known as the land of saints, scholars and leprechauns. In recent years the idea that no saints exist has become almost as popular as the belief that all leprechauns have packed up their bags and gone. Whilst I cannot confess to seeing any saints in modern Ireland I do firmly believe in Leprechauns. Few people in modern Ireland would publicly admit to seeing the little fellows, but many will concede that they have seen them if asked in private. Leprechauns are traditionally reported to have been sighted in rural areas, such as at the edge of a wood in county Wexford, by a loch shore in County Clare or in the ragged regions of the Macgilly-cuddy's reeks, but these mischievous little fellows also make their way into the urban areas of Belfast, Cork and Dublin.

Why is this last fact rarely recognised? Firstly the leprechauns spend their summers and autumns in the country side where the green foliage of summer and the golden foliage of the autumn provide excellent camouflage for the little green clad men with their golden whiskers. Only when winter sets in will the leprechauns seek the warmth of the city. Secondly during the summer and autumn seasons Ireland is filled with American tourists who occasionally bump into the leprechauns. This has two results. First of all the tourists associate the little men with the countryside where they have seen them and secondly few people believe Americans so they stop believing in leprechauns at all. As would be expected, the leprechauns are spotted by many more people during the winter when they move into the cities, but since all the tourists have gone home they are spotted by the indigenous Irish folk who never want to admit to seeing anything unusual, for fear of being accused of being drunk.

I heard a few years ago of a little pub in Belfast which was supposed to be frequented by leprechauns on cold winter nights. Of course like everyone else who heard the story I laughed and forgot about it. However, one cold winter night, close to Christmas as myself and three friends, Mary, John and Charlie, made our way home from work we decided to head to a pub for a warm whiskey.

'Let's try that Leprechaun pub' said one of my friends and so we started out in that direction.

13

When we entered we saw the barman sitting in front of the bar watching television.

'What a shame' we whispered to each other. We really had not expected to see any newfangled equipment in a pub which was rumoured to be frequented by Leprechauns. We ordered our drinks and sat down.

'That's the hottest whiskey I've ever tasted' declared Charlie.

'And that's the sweetest rum that's ever passed my lips,' enthused Mary. Sure enough the drink seemed especially good and before we realised we had taken four drinks each. Mary called the barman over to order another round and only then it struck me that he had curly golden locks and ginger whiskers. I stood up to call him over myself but felt so dizzy that I had to sit down immediately. Just then John collapsed and Charlie jumped to his aid. After a quick examination, Charlie put John's glass to his mouth and wet his lips with the remainder of the drink.

'That's Poteen he was drinking,' roared Charlie after tasting John's drink. 'What on earth do you mean selling that stuff in a public house,' he roared at the barman whilst grabbing him by his whiskers and pulling him over the bar. It was then I noticed that the barman had been standing on a stool all along and was barely two feet tall. The barman caught a pint glass which was sitting on the shelf and threw its entire contents over my friend.

'Damn you,' roared Charlie, releasing his grip on the barman and rubbing the liquid from his eyes. Mary quietly told Charlie to behave, ordered us three more drinks, and sat down, apparently unmoved by the fact that her boyfriend had just collapsed.

'I'm damned if I'm going to make a fuss about him if you're not,' said Charlie as he continued to wipe the drink from his face. Just then a harp player emerged and stood beside the hearth and began playing whilst someone sang a ballad about an old Ulster hero. I immediately felt like dancing but the second I got off my stool my legs turned to butter and I had to sit down once again.

The next thing I knew Mary was being asked out for a dance by the gentleman sitting beside her. She accepted and went to move towards the harp player when he grabbed her hand and said, 'Sure we'll dance here.' He jumped off his stool and stood up on the counter holding Mary's hands while she stood on the floor. At first she was shy, but then she became frightened as she saw that all the men in the pub were gathered around her laughing and cheering. She let go of the little man and pushed him off the counter before grabbing her bag and dashing out.

My friend burst out laughing which met with disapproval from the other men in the pub. He received a punch in the jaw and swung round intending to strike the culprit, but only connected with me. I fell to the floor and the next thing I remember was seeing my two friends John and Charlie who both appeared unconscious being carried out of the pub on the shoulders of tiny men all about two feet tall. I remained in the pub trying not to be noticed and indeed appeared to be successful. The sweet music, the drinking and the laughing continued for about an hour, until a huge policeman entered and told us to go. I decided to go immediately and got down on my hands and knees and tried to creep unnoticed out of the pub. The next thing I knew one of the little men had jumped up on my back and pushed a bottle of whiskey towards my face saying, 'Since you be going home my way you'll give me a lift and I'll let you finish off this bottle of whiskey by way of gratitude.' The pub shook with laughter as I set out on my hands and knees with the bottle of whiskey.

A few hundred yards further on, one of my neighbours was walking along the road and shouted, 'Get up out of that Billy O'Shea crawling along the road in that state with a bottle in your hand.'

'I'm giving this wee fellow on my back a lift home,' I assured him, making a gesture with my thumb.

'You're fit for the mental house,' shouted my neighbour pulling me up and leading me home. It would appear that the little man had jumped off somewhere along the way but no-one was ever going to believe my story. Things only got worse the following morning when I woke up to discover that Charlie's punch had left me with a black eye. It was simply assumed that I was a drunkard. My friends were not about to back up my story either. John had collapsed after drinking four glasses of Poteen and had forgotten everything. Mary was embarrassed at dancing with another man after her boyfriend had collapsed and Charlie was either embarrassed to say anything which could make him appear a drunkard or to admit that he was beaten in a fight with tiny men. In any case neither I nor my friends ever claim that we saw anything unusual that night.

One final word. If any American out there ever dreams of catching the Leprechaun with his crock of gold you had better dispense with the naive idea that the Leprechauns are saintly rural folk and should hurry down to one of the Belfast or Dublin pubs where the Leprechaun's golden money is being swapped for golden liquid at an alarming rate.

Walking Out

by

Laurence J Ogilby

The hiss of the bus doors opening, unscheduled stop, bring me reluctantly from my trance. A glance through the misted window permits a furtive view of camouflaged soldiers aiming weapons into the darkness. The policeman enters, like an overstuffed beetle - complete with flak-jacket - eager to get out from the late October chill. No-matter how routine, one is made instantly alert and privacy is stripped.

I unzip my overnight bag, which merely gets a perfunctory glance and a comment; 'You must read a lot then!'

It does not require an answer although the hard back copy of 'The Deceiver' strikes me as ironic. God! I hate sloppy security. Waiting for the pedestrian lights to acknowledge our existence, I am depressed at the view across the road. The Law Courts in Chichester Street. So many car bombs, the road now sealed off but wait! Let us commission architects to make our security entrenchments pleasing to the eye. But the brain can only conclude this to be merely a concession to a prolonged and insidious war. As I pass the magistrate's court, I recall my presence there some five weeks previous and the withdrawal of my driving licence for a year. My mood does not improve.

Nearing the city centre, I register that it's Thursday and late night shopping. Bright lights and people racing to make those last minute purchases before nine-o'clock, envelope me into much welcomed normalcy. My overnight bag, restricts me from entering any of the stores, as I've already had enough of the big brother security system peering into my affairs. Paranoia becomes a way of life in Belfast.

Just let me absorb the hustle and bustle, watching the consumerholics already engaged in feathering their Christmas nests. Time for a pint!

At the Northern Bank cash-point on York Street, I am aware of a presence behind me but with so many shoppers around and the vigil at the City Hall in support of the recently opened 'Brook Centre' it would be a very desperate mugger to want my thirty quid!

With barely two hours to go before I'm picked up, it's not worth hitting my usual haunts, so turning the corner of May Street the 'Washington' seems an appropriate watering hole. The penquined figure of Neanderthal man stands guard to the entrance, making even me have second doubts as to our ancestry.

'A pint of Guinness please.'

I realise I am reduced to conversing with those in positions of service only. An empty table beckons close to the juke-box and I am already being succumbed by the warmth, cigarette smoke and atmosphere of people keeping life at bay.

Was I always this alone? Of course not. But why had she left?

Yeh, all those others in my work. I didn't really expect so much more. Sure, when the disciplinary hearing came around it would be a matter of procedure.

Shit! Looking after you own ass was an acknowledged degree subject these days. Don't step out of line buddy or we'll nail your hide. A square peg in a round hole - that's me!

God, just half a pint and I'm getting morose.

The juke-box distracts me. The studious looks on faces as they attempt to express their individuality. A glance sideways and the ever present diversion of two neon-illuminated spider's webs to gamble upon.

Back to reality! The seating, table and chair, closer to the floor than the fancy brass hand rail, cutting into my back. My only comfortable position leaves my right foot sticking out into the passage. My apology, however belated goes unacknowledged as seems symbolic of recent months. He seems unconcerned that his shin has just been forcefully obstructed by my foot but then physical contact of any kind is quickly disregarded in these days of inter-personal space. His pint goes on top of the 'Nickelodia' and the freckled face stays impassive as he concentrates upon the odds. Five feet seven, stocky build with red hair, he is the caricature of West Belfast manhood. God, I've worked there long enough and never once asked if I was a Prod. If you were there, you had to be one of them.

Not so on the other side! I can still feel the cold steel on my fore-head as the two hooded youths - Red Hand Commando's scream; 'Keep working with the Taigs and your dead!'

Even this crap I could suffer, but when you're being court martialled for going for a pint on a cross-communtiy weekend with the kids - I had cracked. But there was a common-demoninator - the I.R.A., the U.V.F, and the system - all knelt at the alter of self interest and money.

Shit! Get another pint in.

Lighting my third cigarette at the bar (unemployment benefit will not support previous lifestyles) two attractive, tightly clad 'publicity executives?' are busy erecting display boards to encourage the punters to indulge in free pints, tee-shirts and base-ball caps. Is there no respite from the market economy? Layers within layers.

Back at the table, having sipped into my second pint my attention is inter-rupted by the appearance of another uniformed figure. This time a recruit of the army of God purveying the 'War Cry'. My guilt gathers in my throat as I mutter, 'I've been at war for the past forty two years mate!'

'Do you know Jesus sir?' he asks.

My stare freezes him out.

Maybe I should go round to the Sunday service with a six pack. If I can get the house sold before it's repossessed, maybe I can float a trip back to Israel, to Rosh Pinna. Swop one form of madness for another.

Glancing at my watch, courtesy of Maxol gift coupons, it's nearing half-past ten. The 'Leprechaun' has since been defeated by the logistics of the one-armed bandit and decided to live to fight another day. Why he had to give me such a dirty look as he left is his affair. Perhaps his leg is still hurting! Draining the last of my glass, I decide a visit to the toilet would be advisable before hitting the cold. The old kidneys are not so resilient now.

Zip up - and a quick glance in the mirror. Recognition at least. Yes, I can ac-cept myself.

Memory recall to my last marriage break-up, ten years ago and the stranger looking back at me.

Am I cracking up in my isolation?

More pieces of my personal jig-saw to be sought?

What is gnawing at me?

Shoulder bag. Eyes focused on my overnight bag.

What is it?

Something not right - not fitting.

Think... think.

Let it come. Close your eyes, relax. Succumb to your intuition.

Listen to the inner voice.

Slowly, all the personal garbage evaporates. Existence is defined into the past few hours - army, police, security forces.

That's it! Even for here there's a big flap on.

They've had a tip-off ... something coming down!

He had a bag!

He did! When he came in - he was carrying a sports bag over his shoulder.

He left without it.

Cold freeze.

Entering the bar, I approach the gambling machine. Lodged between it's side and the partition wall, a black imitation leather hold-all - packed with death?

Irrational thoughts of just walk on. Buy another pint and solve all your problems. I look around the packed room, faces, real people sitting through this same real insanity.

For what do we deserve this?

The cause?

Punishment for sins yet to be acknowledged?

Maybe I do deserve it ... but I cannot judge others.

The young bar-man looks perplexed when I tell him, 'There's a bomb in the bar.' I sound too sure. He cannot recall the early seventies. I think he thinks I've planted it!

'For God's sake, get everybody the hell out of here!'

The white cordoning tape seems an insufficient barrier as the army and police attempt to secure the area. Sirens and flashing lights complete the tabloid. Those directly threatened are joined by the inevitable gaggle of passive on-lookers to watch the spectacle, from the side-walk.

Curiosity could kill the cat!

The blast is unbelievable. Pure chaos!

Things which are solid and secure are obliterated into matchsticks and visions of hell.

I look at the shocked and ashen faces around me, contemplating just how thin a line we walk.

My eardrums pound and I can feel my very skeleton rattle within my flesh. My vulnerability neauseates me. I console my self with the knowledge that even though I can take nothing with me into death, nor can my problems follow to haunt me.

Looking over my shoulder, I see Dad's car pulling into Bedford Street, I am relieved - let me out of here.

Opening the passenger door, I sense his distress.

'I heard the explosion. Has anyone been hurt?'

'No. Not this time, they got it cleared just in time.' I reply.

Going out of the city on the motorway, the passing head-lights seem to compete with my racing thoughts.

Sure, I could identify him. But I know there are another hundred waiting to take his place. I recall his stare as he walked out.

Cold and searching.

19

Then I see Liz's face, full of tears and anguish as she walked out.

I rummage for my Walkman, I cannot talk. Pressing play I'm told ' I need a bus-load of faith to get by'. Tell me about it.

Yeh, I'll get by - the alternative does not bear thinking about.

Untitled

by

Marleen Rajan

Funny how close she always felt to Tom on this particular day of the year. Of course, she constantly thought of him: of the things they had done together, of the places they had visited. But today - Remembrance Day - she always felt especially close to him. She'd never forget the day she left him to the station. They'd been so much in love. She had held her tears in check till the train had pulled out - trying to be brave for his sake. Clinging to his uniform lapels, she'd vowed to wait for him. And wait for him she had - until the day postie had pushed his cranky old bike up the cobbled street, and with head solemnly bowed had handed her the telegram. She had known when she saw the black edging that he was dead - *'Missing In Action'* it said, *'Presumed Dead'*. Dead: and with him all their hopes, their plans and dreams. There had been on-one who measured up to him since - and that had been forty-two years ago. She had thrown herself into her work with careless abandon after that, and her free time was spent looking after her frail, aging parents. Her father had died after a long lingering illness and her mother had followed shortly after - their bond of love too strong in life to be broken in death.

So now she was alone. A little old lady who pottered around watering her plants, and keeping her little patch scrubbed and clean. No-one bothered to visit. It seemed as if nobody cared. Today as she busied herself, eating a meagre breakfast and donning her best suit, she felt suddenly very old, very unloved. She wondered how much longer she would have to carry on. She ached for Tom: longed to be with him, comforted by him.

Closing her front door, she stopped to pick a dew-kissed rose from her well-tended garden. She walked briskly, her cheeks glowing in the biting wind, her head full of Tom. Her footsteps led her to the cemetery. Kneeling there, she tenderly and reverently placed the rose on her parents' grave.

Sprinkling the velvet petals with her tears, she stood in lonely repose. There was no grave for Tom this side of the British Channel. His body lay under a foreign sky. No rose of remembrance rested on his grave. Slowly, silently, she turned and walked the short distance into town.

There was an air of dignified solemnity hanging over the square. The War Memorial stood proud and erect: a rallying point for the people of the town to honour those who had given their all so that civil and religious liberty would be the right of every citizen. The military band could be heard slowly making its way to the Cenotaph. People were starting to line the streets. Today they were united in gathering to honour their forebearers; their respect and reverence was almost a tangible thing. It hung in the still squared shoulders of the old veterans; it stood in the military bearing of today's fresh young soldiers - so innocent for all their rigorous training. Tom had been innocent once - and so young.

'They shall grow not old. . .' the clergyman intoned. She felt an old familiar tap on her shoulder. Turning round, her look of startled surprise was quickly replaced by a warm, glowing smile. Through misty eyes, she felt it fitting that he should be here by her side today. Eagerly, she slipped her small childlike hand into his stronger grasp. No longer would she feel alone, uncared for and unloved.

Around her, a small circle had gathered. One of the town's dignitaries bowed his head when he saw what had happened.

'Ach, it's Miss Rose,' he sighed, 'Wee Miss Rose. She's slipped away to be with her Tom at last.'

Sabena

by

Florence Lyster

Yor lords, your ladies, your graces, I be old Sabena, Duchess of the Highways. I wanders from one town in Ireland to another, from Kerry to Dublin to Belfast, bringing with me good will and cross breedin' of fleas. But there's no place in Ireland I love better than here in Carricknure, all the more so because every year they have the most wonderful Drama Festival, with prizes for everything. There's a big silver sugar bowl for the best actor, a canteen of cutlery for the best actress, and a fine big shiny leather boot for the best bawlin' and shoutin' producer in all Ireland.

But the most prestigious award of all is the Pewter Bull for Dramatic Oratory, hotly contested for every year, on a perennial basis, by two of the town's most forthstanding citizens. . . for the one corner, Rory Fergal O'Shane, the resident magistrate, and for the other. . . John Knox Montgomery, the town physician.

But last year a terrible disaster happened, for the fellow who was supposed to brief the adjudicator on the traditions of the festival got mixed up in a football match and forgot to do so, with the result that the Pewter Bull for Dramatic Oratory was awarded to Rory Fergal O'Shane for the second year running.

It was only after they'd got the adjudicator safely on the train and on the way back to the airport that the real conquest for the Pewter Bull began. Rory O'Shane was a man not greatly noted for tact or modesty, and he took out round the town with the Bull, accompanied by all the bands and banners he could find. He even had the temerity to break into the local Orange Hall and borrow the big Lambeg drum. Conspicuous by their absence were the supporters of John Knox Montgomery, but we'll hear about them fellows when we get round the corner.

The whole town was out watching the procession and the children were leaning out of the top windows to see the show. It all went well until they came to Bullock's Field, and there the men of Montgomery were lying in ambush. Then truly began the Battle of the Pewter Bull. The red rays of the setting sun shone on the raw hides of the men of Montgomery and O'Shane as they kicked and clouted and verbally abused each other. And there at one end of the field, raised on a dias, with eyes like the heart of a volcano, a thunderstorm on its brow and its great horns silhouetted against the night sky, rose the Pewter Bull for Dramatic Oratory. Sure 'twas like a mighty God of the East gazing upon the red dome of the setting sun as it rested upon Mount Fergal.

And the men of Montgomery and O'Shane fought bravely on into the hours of darkness, until all of a sudden, over the crest of the hill came the greatest peace keeping force in Ireland. It was headed by Gabriel Reynolds, Commandant of the Guardai, and John Henderson, Chief Constable of the R.U.C.

And behind them were representatives of every religious and secular order in Ireland. There was the Charismatic Order, the Orange and Black Orders, the Doctors' Orders the New World Order and three Russian observers on a troika. And they were all carrying torches and lanterns; sure 'twas like the moonlight glinting and capering on a mountain stream. And at the sight of it the men of Montgomery and O'Shane tore into this place of public hospitality and they laid down their arms on that bar counter there for a draught of Bass Guinness. After an hour or so of this they swore that never again would they go to war over the Pewter Bull. With what little wit they had left to them they decided to split the Bull in two and give one half to O'Shane and the other half to Montgomery. They would drive the Daimler of John Montgomery and the Mercedes of Fergal O'Shane back to back and attach the forelegs of the Bull to one bumper and the hind legs to the other, and drive them apart. But the Pewter Bull, like the Old Orange Flute was indestructible, and it was more by a nod and a wink from the Almighty than by pure coincidence that the Bull arrived, a dislocated bumper at either end of it, at the feet of the only person left standing fit to make a decision of any kind, Sister Augusta McGuiness. And that good lady decreed that from then on the Pewter Bull for Dramatic Oratory should remain in a special niche in this place of public hospitality and that each year the name of the winner should be suspended between the horns of the Bull.

And if every word I've told you be not the God's honest truth, may I never live to tell you another lie.

The Matchmaker

by

Katy Connell

It was the mammy who decided that the time had come for Marty to get married. She had been ill and had to go to live with her daughter. Life on the farm was too much for her now, but before she went she engaged the Matchmaker to find a wife for Marty, a strong young woman who would look after him and work on the farm as well, not too young but not too old either. The mammy gave the Matchmaker clear instructions, told Marty what she'd done, then left for her daughter's home with an easy mind. This was rural Ireland a long time ago.

Marty missed the mammy even though he was always busy on the farm and went to see her every week. It was lonely now, he lived in such an isolated place with only the dogs for company, especially as the winter had set in early. He was glad that the mammy had gone to the Matchmaker for him. He had been only too happy to agree to an arranged marriage. It was the accepted custom in those remote and lonely parts. Anyway he was by nature a quiet man, not used to socialising. There was no other way he'd find a wife.

The Matchmaker was Mr McGonigle the village schoolmaster. He had inherited the job from his uncle who still acted as adviser. There was not much the pair of them didn't know about the history of the families for miles around, the uncle being expert on the older generation, many of whose marriages he had arranged, and Mr McGonigle knowing the younger ones most of whom he had taught at some time or other in the village school. Because of this expert knowledge, and some good old fashioned common sense in matching the right people to one another, they had become highly proficient at the job. It was a privilege to find your life's partner with the help of Mr McGonigle. That was why the mammy had gone to him. He was the best there was.

It was arranged for Marty to go to see Mr McGonigle as well of course. So one bright frosty afternoon he got the pony and trap out and drove down to the village. Mr McGonigle was seated in a comfortable armchair in front of a great big fire piled high with turf, in the front room of his cottage. The air was filled with the smell of freshly baked bread and a hint of the Irish stew they had had for their dinner. Mrs McGonigle, a homely woman, was feeding the baby in the

25

kitchen. Seeing this warm homely scene unfolding about him made the lonely Marty long for a wife too. The mammy had only been gone for a short time, but she had not been fit for a long time, and it had been hard to work the farm and look after the home as well. Marty told the Matchmaker he would like to get settled as soon as possible.

'Sure I've been looking around for you since the mammy spoke to me,' he said, 'and I think I've found someone who might suit. She's a lovely big girl, 35 years old but don't let that put you off.'

'What does she look like?' asked Marty as most men would. 'Is she good looking?'

'Well it all depends on what you mean by good looking,' Mr McGonigle replied. 'She's more healthy looking than pretty if you know what I mean.' And he showed Marty a picture of a sturdy no nonsense country girl. 'She's a good cook and a grand worker and she knows all about farms,' he continued. 'She's been keeping house for her brother but he has just got married. Sure I arranged that match myself. She's got to leave the house now. What do you think? Will I have a word with her about you?'

Marty had nothing to lose so he said 'Yes.'

In his heart he was pleased that someone had been found already, and not only that, this young woman needed a home. She would be grateful to Marty if it all worked out. He wouldn't have to try too hard. Marty had not been at all sure that it would be easy to find a wife even with the expert help of Mr McGonigle.

So a meeting was arranged. They met for tea with Mr and Mrs McGonigle in their cottage. It was part of the service. They got on remarkably well from the word go. Then Marty took the young woman, whose name was Clare, on an outing and that really decided him. Clare would suit well. It was an exceedingly brief courtship. He needed a wife housekeeper. She needed a home. They liked one another well enough, neither expected a great romance. There was no time to waste on either side. Marty had made up his mind. After first taking her to meet the mammy and his sisters and getting their approval, he proposed and she accepted. They had been well matched.

Then Clare said there was just one thing. She had a twin sister. If she married him this twin sister would have to come and live with them, she needed a home too. If he wouldn't agree to this they would call the marriage off. Marty felt by now that Clare was his big chance and he didn't want to lose her. He might not meet anyone like her again. She was a strong competent woman who reminded him vividly of his mother in her heyday. She even had the look of his mother.

He had no idea what it felt like to be in love. All those years on that isolated farm he had come into contact with few women, but he did feel a certain warmth towards Clare, a feeling he had never experienced in all his 45 years. So Marty agreed. He was basically a kind man. And the twin would always be an extra hand on the farm.

Marty and Clare took their marriage vows must before Christmas. There was no honeymoon of course. That was not the custom at that time in that part of the world. Marty and Clare drove back to the farm after the ceremony and a week later the twin sister joined them bringing all the sisters' worldly possessions with her. Everyone approved. It had all worked out so well. The marriage consummated, the Matchmaker was paid his fee. Clare didn't come cheap. The fee was based on the size of the farm. Marty was comfortably off with a good bit of land and a milking herd. This was all taken into account. But as time went by Marty realised that Clare had been worth every penny. He had done very well for himself. A year later the first child arrived, a fine healthy boy and for this Mr McGonigle received his final payment.

The gossip started up after the second son was born. Marty and the twins were always together. When he came down to the village or up to town for supplies they would be with him, one on each arm. Since the twins were identical no one could tell which twin was the wife, and they appeared to encourage this. Inevitably people speculated whether Marty could tell them apart, or were they both acting in the capacity of wife. Several more sons were born and daughters too, but as the midwife said, she couldn't tell the twins one from the other. But the gossip didn't seem to touch the family. They lived happily ever after on their remote farm.

The gossip reached the mammy of course in the way gossip does. At first she was shocked at the rumours, but then said firmly that she didn't believe a word of it and that was the end of the matter. Her son was happy and that was all that mattered to her. No-one argued with the mammy.

Mr McGonigle had the last word on the matter. He believed in families, he said. Who would dare to begrudge this family their happiness in one another, and in the children. There was little enough love in the world. All right so it had started out with little emotion but where there's no love put love and you'll find love. 'Tis what he always said.

Then he got out his bicycle to ride up the mountain to pay the Byrne Brothers a visit. They could only afford one wife. He thought he had found a solution to their problem. He believed passionately in home and family and people being a comfort to one another.

'That's what we're put on this earth for', he'd say and he was doing his bit in helping those unable to achieve this for themselves.

Parisian Nightmare

by

Jean Withers

Nicole stepped off the Champs-Elysees into the open fronted bar, peering anxiously into the unaccustomed shade. She picked her way through the chairs arranged in serried ranks enabling the clientele to enjoy the passing throng. Her eyes impatiently scanned and rejected each occupant. The tenseness in her face was out of place in these casual surroundings, as was her immaculate city suit.

Then she caught sight of him, settled in a booth in the inner shop. In an instant the worry lines gave way to a smile, and the veil of anxiety lifted from her grey eyes. The sight of him was like water to a parched plant. She crossed to him quickly, put her arm on his shoulder and bent to kiss the face he turned to her.

'Mon Cheri', she smiled. She drew her fingers gently along the line of his jaw. 'I am so happy to see you.'

She sat down opposite him and as she chatted animately her hungry eyes were taking in every detail of his being - his lean tanned hands and carefully manicured nails, his beautifully tailored suit, the gold cuff-links she had given him for their first Christmas together.

Her search lingered on the greying hairs above his ears and the crinkle lines around his eyes. Her stomach lurched with longing. But when she met his gaze - cool, uninterested, distant - the lurching settled to a heavy cold weight somewhere deep inside her. She swallowed hard, and knew this was no nightmare that was going to end when she opened her eyes. This was for real.

She spoke faster now, ignoring the presence of the waiter. There was a forced brightness in her voice as she told him of all the things that happened to her since they last met, that morning. Perhaps if she poured enough words into the chasm between them she would eventually reach him. She touched his hand tentatively and he withdrew it, slowly and deliberately.

Her gaunt crimson tipped fingers lifted a wrapped sugar lump from the dish on the table. Nervously she turned it over and over, just as she was churning this dilemma over and over in her mind while her mouth persisted with its unconnected chatter. She stopped as she caught sight of the tiny, delicately drawn iris on one side of the wrapper. She wanted to scream. Irises had been 'their'

29

flowers, and had meant as much to them as single red roses meant to so many other couples.

She forced herself to set the sugar down, on the saucer of his empty coffee cup. Her index finger traced the rim and she felt the kiss of his lips in every fibre of her body. She turned to him again, her pleading eyes darting fitfully over his face, his hands and his chest, but avoiding direct contact with his icy blue stare.

The waiter brought the cognac he had ordered for her. It had barely touched the red gingham table cover before she grasped the glass tightly and lifted it quickly to her lips. She downed it in one, hardly ceasing her monologue to do so. He ordered another, watching her closely but dispassionately, completely untouched by the desperate warmth and the frantic energy she exuded.

By the time she had thrown back her fourth cognac he could detect the sweat glistening on her brow; he saw her eyes narrow in comtemptive dismissal. He watched her upper lip curl as she threw insults at him, interspersed with the abject apology of the drunk. Her jacket was askew and her skirt had ridden up her thighs as she slid lower in her seat. Even the long tanned legs which had captivated him for so long had no power to rescue her from the unattractive pose.

Her voice was raised now as she included the other patrons of the bar in her vilification of this man who had so betrayed her - she, who had given him everything; he who would share only a tiny corner of his life with her.

He was aware of the interest shown by other customers in this colourful revelation of their relationship. Some were furtive and embarrassed while others were openly admiring, whether of him or her he could not be sure. It was time to go.

With detached deliberation he rose from the table, enshrouded still by the venomous mantle issuing from the smudged red slash that was her mouth.

He took her firmly by the elbow and raised her almost bodily from her seat. He had to hold her while she scrabbled under the table for her bag. Despite her loud protestations and feeble attempts to shake him off, he guided her unsteady figure back into the twilight of the Champs-Elysees. The passers-by opened a way for them before they were swallowed up in the anonymity of the crowd.

He studied her as she lay on the bed, still unmade from their encounter the previous night. The duvet cover with its printed irises was lumpy and wrinkled. With her soft hair spread unkempt across the pillow, and her features relaxed as in dreamless sleep, he was momentarily reminded by a stirring deep in his soul of what they had once shared together.

30

No sooner had the memory taken flight than it was savagely grounded and crushed to death by all the other, more recent remembrances. His eyes hardened again as he recalled her drunken phone calls to his office and to his home; her attempts to own him body and soul; her inability to accept and enjoy what had meant so much to them for several years. He was angry at the waste of it all.

He had come last night in a final attempt to end it, to stop the sickening vacillation between overwhelming desire for her, and disgust at the drunken harridan she was becoming more and more frequently. But he had not been strong enough and he had allowed himself to be seduced, again.

Even before he had opened his eyes that morning he had known, from the scent of her nearness, where he was. In that moment he hated himself almost as much as he hated her.

He had slipped out of bed and dressed quickly and quietly, anxious to put as much distance between them as possible. Only as he was leaving did she stir.

'James?' she said softly.

'Good-bye, ma Cherie', he had replied before closing the door behind him.

Not 'au revoir' - till we meet again - but the much more final, formal, English 'good-bye'. Last night he had meant to make the parting as painless as possible and there it was, cleanly and viciously, in one word- 'Goodbye' - like a steel rapier, straight to the heart.

The effect of the single English word was not lost on Nicole. She knew instinctively that he was withdrawing from their relationship in which he always spoke her language, the language of love. She had called after him, but to no avail.

She dressed hurriedly, not even taking time to wash, anxious only that she should find a way to reach him again. She downed a couple of cognacs to help her think straight.

She phoned his office a number of times early in the day, and was informed that he had an external appointment and was not expected until mid-morning. She cancelled an important meeting of her own at 10.30 so that she would definitely be available when James called. She poured a drink, so that she might be calm, and self assured.

She made the phone call herself, at 10.35, just to make sure he had got the message. She did not know that every call to his office that day - blocked by his secretary, but reported to him - steeled his resolve against her. When eventually he spoke to her and arranged to meet her later that afternoon she per-

suaded herself that his apparent coolness was due to someone else's presence in the
office.

She wished she had time to go home to change, but she took extra care with her make-up, having a few drinks from the office cabinet to steady her hand.

'Lynette', she called through to her secretary, 'Would you order another bottle of cognac please?' Nicole was too busy putting up her long blonde hair to notice the raised eyebrow.

By the time she entered the bar on the Champs-Elysees she had forgotten the word 'good-bye' - she only knew there was an uncertain tension between them that she would charm away.

Not any more he thought. A sad smile twisted his lips. Tomorrow he would wake in his own bed and know that his nightmare was over. He gave not a thought to the nightmare that had begun when he covered her face with the iris-strewn pillow.

'Goodbye, ma Cherie,' he said softly as he closed the door behind him for the last time.

Dying to Work

by

Alex Lee Parsey

Jane turned over in the darkness beneath the cotton duvet her movement creating a light draught which cooled her knees. She glanced for what seemed the hundredth time at the green illuminated figures on the radio alarm clock. Twelve twenty three glowed back at her. Tom was much later than usual, but then he always went for a few drinks on Friday evening with his work mates. Even so, he had never been this late before without telephoning home.

The sound of a dog barking outside crashed into the room. It made her concentrate to listen for footsteps that didn't exist. Every evening had become the same. Waiting alone for the sound of Tom's key in the lock; fear turning her flesh cold; dread that this time the door would be knocked and opened to a police uniform.

It had only been four months since John Neal had been shot. He had been Tom's closest friend. In fact they had both started their jobs together on the same day. She remembered how she had begged Tom not to take the carpenters job with Harry Monrow's firm. It was notorious for taking on construction work in so called 'Bad areas'. The firm sent their mixed work force into hard line estates regardless of their religion. The fact that Monrow's boasted a mixed work force in the first place was worth boasting about, but to insist that they become potential murder victims to prove an absence of religious bigotry was lunacy.

She would never forget the morning she found Tom in that hospital corridor, slumped forward only half occupying the hard orange plastic chair with his hands clasped together in white knuckled despair. As she had approached him he had lifted his head to expose reddened eyes like blood dripped onto a white pillow. She thanked God he was still alive; that she could look back into his hurt and know he would recover.

The cooling corpse of John Neal lay heavy and lifeless on a gelid steel trolley while his wife tried to squeeze breath back into his naked body, hugging gaping wounds no longer able to bleed. Jane could hear her own fearful voice in John's wife's screams while Tom lowered his head again to cover his ears against her pain. The evening news showed pictures of yet another coffin on the day John was buried. One more wooden box carried with solemnity through the streets of Ulster.

One of the children coughing in the next bedroom brought her thoughts back into the darkened room. She felt cold now and wished even more that Tom was laying next to her, his warm breath reassuring on the back of her neck. The clock told her only a few moments had passed, yet it seemed much longer since her last look at the time. Memories and visions flashed through her mind so rapidly she could not hold any one image long enough on which to focus. As her agitation grew she began to fidget with her wedding ring turning it around and around on her finger as was her habit when nervous.

It had been just nine years since Tom had placed the plain gold band on her finger although to her it represented a life time. Jane could barely remember not being with Tom. They had dated since their teens; got engaged after a couple of years and married two years after that. There had been nothing exceptional in their courtship. No great rush of passion like one reads about in romantic novels. Just a firm steady relationship that grew with familiarity and progressed in the way everyone expected. Their two children were planned almost with military precision like everything else in their lives. Nothing caught them unawares. Perhaps mundanity had exaggerated her fears for Tom's safety, warped her interpretation of the situation. But then just how warped was every other sectarian murder in the province. How many knew or believed that they were at risk. What was the percentage of men who when confronted by that last strangers face were prepared to feel that piece of lead smash into their skulls before lights out. It was too easy to become a target.

Jane tried to picture Tom in her mind chatting with his friends. His broad northern accent filling a room, enlivening it with infectious laughter. She tried to place him in some sort of environment that sparkled with vitality and life. By imagining him vociferous and animated she kept him alive. Yet, the stark image of his body prostrate on the muddy ground of a building site or at the edge of a lonely road side seeped into her thoughts and refused to budge. It suffocated every other vision she tried to conjure up until she wanted to cry out in her panic.

A car door slamming against the silence promised false hope until a neighbours gate rattled closed. A surge of hatred for the neighbour overwhelmed her, closely followed by self disgust. She could not believe how stupid she was being. How could she have become so ridiculously unreasonable. She hated a man because he was home safely. A feeling of shame swelled within her like a glass balloon, expanding until it shattered, its shards stabbing her into anger.

Patience exhausted, she swung her bare legs into the chilled air and pulled on a woollen dressing gown.

The white china mug, stippled with tiny red hearts, warmed her hands as she grasped it tightly between her palms. The street lighting outside shone palely on the small front garden as she stood in the darkened lounge peering out through the slightly opened curtain.

Jane pulled an armchair closer to the window and wrapped her dressing gown tightly around her in flimsy protection before settling back into the soft cushion. At least in this position she could hear the chink of the front gate when Tom came home. She could meet him at the front door and feel his arms around her, his leather jacket cool and damp from the night air against her body reassuring her.

The warmth from the tea and the constant staring into nothingness nudged Jane into sleep. Not a restful sleep, but a disturbing fitful sleep that turned dream into reality and anxiety into terror.

Tom glanced into his rearview mirror and was almost blinded as the glaring headlights of a car travelling behind him reflected brightly in the glass. The car drew up close to Tom's car bumper, braked, drifted back a small distance, then drew up close again. Panic forced Tom's foot harder onto the accelerator pedal while the dark coloured car effortlessly kept pace. He drove faster, terror gripping his chest until he almost forgot to breathe. Sweat swelled and cooled on Tom's upper lip and forehead. A rigidity seemed to urge his muscles into altering his previously smooth gear changes into jerking frantic movements as he drove faster and faster along the winding rural road.

The sudden loss of control as he plunged through a roadside hedge spun him, in what felt like slow motion, through the air. His only desire that the car cease turning over so he could run before his pursuers had time to reach him. Blue flashes caused by the jarring from the crash began to fade inside his head as the car rested on its side, the wheels still spinning redundantly through the momentarily silent air.

Harsh voices suddenly surrounded him as he struggled up and out through the passenger door. Somewhere in the back of his mind he was aware of a numbness in his left leg, but he was even more aware of the urgent shouts of; 'Find the bastard' closing in around him. As he jumped down into the field his foot buckled under his weight and caused him to stumble. The thud of his body hitting the ground seemed to make a tremendous noise in the stillness. Even his own heart beating became deafening to him as he tried to run across the field without making any noise.

A sound Tom had never heard before echoed through his head as a bullet thwacked into the back of his leather jacket. He was still running when a second bullet drove him to the ground. The iced dew from the grass seeped into his trousers as he sank down onto his knees before toppling sideways to stare up into the clear black sky.

A strangers face hovered above him, peering down at his desperate pleading while a gun barrel loomed huge in front of his right eye. The last words Tom heard were; 'Do it' before the bitter taste of vomit hit the back of his throat.

Tea slurped over the side of the china mug onto Jane's dressing gown as she bolted upright in her chair, Tom's face before her dirty and bloody and mutilated. She felt the cold droplets of sweat trickle down from under her arms to slide like ice along the sides of her stomach. Her dream now cold reality.

An urgent knocking at the front door startled her into motion. Jane stood in the dimly lit hallway and trembled as she turned back the latch. A radio crackled incoherently on a uniformed breast and two unfamiliar faces donned the sympathy guise as one quietly asked; 'Mrs Forrest? Mrs Thomas Forrest? May we come in?'

The Old Coach Road

by

Alfred N Laing

It was a beautiful summer's evening when Alf left the locker-room of Tandragee golf club with his golf bag slung over his shoulder. This was his first year at the club and he preferred to go out in the evening to hack round a few holes and possibly improve his game. On his way he met one of the club's senior members who was returning to the clubhouse on completion of his round. The old boy stopped and introduced himself to Alf commentating on Alf going out so late. Alf just smiled and nodded.

'Don't be going as far as the old coach road.' The old boy said, as he trudged off towards the clubhouse.

Alf shook his head and smiled to himself, then filling his lungs with clean country air he set off towards the eighth hole. Striding out across the tree lined fairways with the smell of newly mown grass in his nostrils was Alf's idea of relaxation, away from the pressures and hassle of business. The Rhododendron bushes flushed against the backdrop of greenery set a beautiful screen, suddenly a large hare broke from cover startling Alf. It's a long time since I've seen a hare, he thought to himself, then a family of rabbits scurried into the safety of the bushes.

On his arrival at the eighth tee Alf took a few balls out of his bag, looked around to see if all was clear, he didn't want a member seeing him hitting practice shots onto the green, as this was against the rules; there were more rules in golf than any other sport he knew of.

The eighth hole is the shortest hole on the course being about 100 meters which Alf could barely reach with an eight iron. He hit all the balls he had with him three times at the green and managed to get half of them onto the green, a few ended up in the bushes with the rest falling around the periphery. One ball landed a foot from the pin and that made Alf's night, so when he had gathered all the balls he sat down on his golf bag and rested his back against a spruce tree, he was beginning to ache after the exertions of swinging the club.

Alf gazed out over the course and his eyes followed the old winding coach road which dissolved into the twilight toward the ancient citadel. He had enquired about the castle when he first joined the club and had been informed

37

that it has once belonged to an English Lord, but now it was part of a potato crisp factory.

As the light faded he could just make out the modern factory jutting out of the side of the old castle like a terrible after thought.

A chilling mist seemed to engulf Alf as he enjoyed his rest. Suddenly a cry startled him.

'Help me! Please help me.'

Alf jumped to his feet and strained his eyes, trying to see in the thickening mist. The cry came from the direction of the old coach road, Alf cautiously approached with his eight iron gripped tightly in his hand. Out of the swirling mist he identified an out stretched hand; again the voice pleaded.

'Help me!' ....

'Help me!'..............

An unfamiliar noise startled Alf and a feeling of dread swamped him, as he realized the sound was that of thundering hooves.

Alf made a grab for the outstretched hand and pulled the entity clear and in the process received a blow from the shoulder of the leading horse which knocked him to the ground. He got to his feet and still holding his eight iron he staggered on down the old coach road.

As he made his way along the road he noticed the outline of what appeared to be a man carrying a staff.

Suddenly four small shadowy figures leaped out of the trees and attacked the man. He cried out brandishing his stick in an effort to fight off his attackers. Alf gave a yell and swinging his club ran to the rescue. Two of the figures turned away from the man to face his attack.

The creatures were about three feet tall with pointed ears, their fluorescent blue eyes shone through oval slits in their leathery skinned faces, and their little pointed teeth pushed prominently over thin, saliva covered lips. In their hands they carried long triple hooks.

Alf almost stopped in his tracks the creatures looked so hideous, but his courage overcame his fear and he struck out with the golf club, knocking the misshapen head completely off the first little horror. A stream of blue fluorescent liquid squirted out from the decapitated creatures neck and a repulsive smell of death filled the air. The second creature caught Alf's jacket with it's hook and with surprising strength began to drag him towards the trees.

'Don't let it get you into the trees,' the man screamed.

Alf looked over and saw that the man's staff had broken, he still had a piece in his hand, the other was imbedded in the chest of one of his attackers.

Alf dug his heels into the road, but even his studded golf shoes couldn't stem the force of the evil entity as it dragged him along the road. He struck out with his club but the little creature dodged his efforts with unforeseen agility. Alf gave up his struggle and let himself be pulled to the edge of the twisted trees, then unexpectedly he kicked out tearing the attacker's face off with the studs of his golf shoe, the creature howled and released its hold on him then Alf killed it with one fatal blow to the head. With his attackers vanquished, he went to the aid of the man who had warned him, he was almost off the road when Alf struck out with his weapon, beheading the devilish creature.

'That's a formidable weapon you have there, I must thank you for saving me,' the stranger said huskily.

'Tell me where the hell I am?' Alf implored the stranger.

'Where indeed, you have passed into the time of lost souls; there are few of us left, most have been dragged off by those demons, others have been crushed under the wheels of the Devil's coach. Our only hope is to persuade someone on the other side to pull us through the barrier into the land of the living, that is our only hope. The unfortunate one who helps you through the barrier is doomed to take your place. I was pulled through several years ago while out walking my dog, I had been warned not to walk this way, but I ignored the warning; now I must tramp this unending road until I can encourage someone to take my place. There's always a warning given, by one who knows.'

Alf thought back to the old golfer who had spoken to him when he had left the clubhouse, he had given him the warning.

'What of the creatures with the hooks?' Alf inquired, he was on the verge of collapse by now.

'They are the evil ones soldiers known as the Procurers, they drag souls off into the depths of hell. You saved me from this fate. If you hadn't come alone I would have been taken.'

A sense of dread crept over Alf as he polished the head of his stainless steel golf club. He had to force himself to look at his own reflection.

'Noooooooo!' He screamed until his lungs hurt. The face he saw in the moon-light wasn't his. Then he blacked out.

'What's all the bloody noise about?' The light from the gamekeepers torch shone into Alf's terrified eyes.

'There's been some poachers around, stealing the young pheasants, and I was just passing on my way to the castle grounds. You can't play golf in the dark, I don't know, talk about fanatics.'

'But .... but ....' then Alf realized he was back on the golf course, I must have dosed off, he thought to himself.

Alf gazed across the course; sure enough bathed in moonlight stood the club-house. He gripped the man's hand and shook it vigorously, then still dazed he walked off into the darkness. The thought of warning the gamekeeper crossed his mind, so he shouted back into the gloom. 'Stay off the old coach road.'

'Old wives tales,' came the reply.

Alf hadn't gone but a few paces when the cold mist closed in behind him and he heard the faint cry.

'Help me! Please help me!'

He took to his heels and as he ran he remembered what the stranger said to him in the dream.

'You always get a warning from one who knows.'

And he had just warned the gamekeeper. Alf didn't stop running until he reached his car..............

Getting Away From Books

by

Julian Boyle

'Listen, I feel a great night is on its way and it's at the door right now, just waiting to get in. We're all gonna get numb, right? I'm gonna go for a circular walk now fellas, on my way to the bar and I'll see what I can rustle up for you.'

As he left, Jack could feel a whole, untapped mine leave with him; it was as if the light above them had stopped working and they became shaded and formless to the room. They sipped their drinks and watched Gerry pass through the crowd. Every couple of steps girls he knew would pull his elbow and drag him gently to their table where he could be as pleasant or rude as he liked. Girls would do anything to please him, perhaps even allow themselves to be guided towards other boys just to form a link. Then another little group would light up in another corner and he would billow over and illuminate. He was a teachers' pet who grasped people quickly like a clever student grasps facts but often the grasp was a snatch which never held anything for long; the quick learner who quickly forgot. Jack felt insulted that he was part of the scheme for it was a public acknowledgement of his own failure with girls. He passed it off as boys fun on a night out, but he knew Gerry was in earnest and in a sense so was he. Molloy and Stelfox were along for the ride, Jack left for the toilet; (a girl stands smoking by the hand-drier. He apologies and runs out, thinking he's in the wrong toilet. He goes into an adjoining door and a great scream goes up. This is the ladies so he runs back into the gents and locks himself into a cubicle. Meanwhile Gerry comes in, glances at the girl and carries on unperturbed. She starts playing with the condom machine and puts money in. She begins to blow on one and then leaves).

Jack returns and Gerry's words came in as the beers went down; 'I'll use my power to help you. I will work miracles for you and help you out of your mess. Everything that comes to you will come through me because I possess the most valuable and the most beautiful gift that there is. Not the ability to splash colours onto canvas, put it in a frame and call it art, nor the ability to kick a ball or any of the other talents that compete for newspaper space. My gift goes further than that for it doesn't rely on outside objects like tennis racquets or even a pen and paper. It is this simple and this profound; I have the ability to

41

reach people, to connect into their emotions and tap them. I can reach right inside people and affect the way they actually feel and so affect their conscious and subconscious states. In short I can draw them towards me and make them fall in love with me. I know how to find people for myself but now I want to use my gift to help others who don't have the natural advantages that I have - people like you Jack; shadow dwellers. I see the way girls look at you, their eyes touched with pity and contempt. Pity is the enemy! Destroy it quickly and surely. If you become the object of pity for a girl, she will never be attracted to you. But that you already know - you can't change yourself completely. I offer you the easy way. I want you to stay exactly the way you are and I will do all the work. I simply propose to transfer all my sexual potency to you. I want to go further than before; not simply persuading her but actually reaching in and directing her feelings from the inside, away from me and towards you. Call it a form of sexual hypnosis. I want her to fall in love with you but through me. Does that make any sense? God, I could have anyone but I want no-one and that's the worst predicament to be in.' Jack nodded in agreement to his own thoughts and came back to the room and his friends again. He leaned towards Stelfox who was small and nervous and didn't have to be impressed; 'Men are threatened by aggressive women and women hate feminine qualities in a man. That makes a nonsense of the idea that women are more thoughtful and considerate than men; for instance shyness in a girl is a virtue; it suggests modesty and sensitivity. In a man it suggests weakness, awkwardness, stupidity, laziness, inhibition, timidity, fear, lack of will power, leadership ideas, and creativity - sheep like qualities generally. All because it is seen as a female trait. On the other side men don't like women who can beat them at tennis.'

Stelfox and Molloy nodded and Stelfox began; 'I think I know what you mean. I used to know a girl; Janet; she was a real beatnik, gothic girl with big DM boots up to her knees and dyed black hair. She was so beautiful and deep and everything. You know, I did everything right with that girl; I was attentive, charming, and oozed wit. Before she did he English GCSE, I lent her my favourite volume of Scott Fitzgerald short stories and my Alan Ladd Great Gatsby video - a prized possession. I told her I loved purple lipstick and the lilac streaks in her hair and that I listened to Curve. I had her in the palm of my hand. Last Easter she got her left nostril pierced with a silver stud so I immediately asked her how she managed to pick her nose. It was a hilarious remark. When I got the video back, it played two episodes of 'Home and Away'. I never saw 'Bernice bobs her hair' again, although the other stories were still there, beginning on page 47.'

'Hmmm; yeah?'

'Carol loved poetry' added Molloy, 'and English and stories and all that. She was always saying that she liked Yeats and had a crush on Shelleys rhyming couplets. In fact she once said that of all the poets there wasn't one she didn't love for she understood the yearning and torment of a poets heart. Last June I wrote her a poem; she hasn't spoken to me since.'

Just then Gerry appeared with a girl at his side.

'Here's someone I'd like you to meet. Caroline, this is Jack, the one I was telling you about.'

'I know it's dark,' she began, 'But were you in the ladies room ten minutes ago?'

With a wave of the hand Gerry had played his part and joined the other two. It was just like Jack to do something like that but she seemed to find it quite funny. Most girls wouldn't - he credited the success to himself. Before long he was pulled away into another group and when he returned half an hour later he was met with two young people, eyes wide and falling in love.

For really the first time in Jacks life, something had happened to him. He hadn't had to pull or push or tear at anything until it fell apart because, as they sat there, events simply took over; decent, friendly forces began to work and before he knew it the whole swirling room disappeared into a kiss. For the previous five minutes he had asked all the usual dumb questions like 'Are you still at school?' Which always brought on swift failure. The answer was no. She was at Queens, studying maths. He told her she must be smart, which was the right thing to say. Here he was, at last, on the winning side and for a reason he couldn't really understand. He hadn't planned or earned this victory yet here he was sharing in the spoils and smiling. She was pretty with green eyes, brown hair and she spoke with a sweet shyness. Her friends came over now and again and knelt beside her and whispered in her ear. She was popular in a sincere, steady way. Someone to love and to like too and she never once moved away. He became her focus and priority.

Then Gerry came back and shouted in his ear; 'Easy! Do you like her? Jesus, I never thought it would be so easy. Did you find some charm or were you just as awkward as usual?'

Rather than feeling grateful. Jack wanted to push his leering face into the balcony. The whole thing was a rotten set up, a snare which Gerry had set and he, Jack, had stolen from. His mood changed and he felt rigid and uncomfortable.

'Why do you like me?' he asked Caroline with a stinging awkwardness and tried to smooth it by adding; 'It's an awful, personal question that I shouldn't have asked but......'

Uncomfortableness transmits faster than electricity and she snapped at him. 'What makes you think I like you at all? Maybe we're both drunk, maybe the lights are too dim. I hardly know you. In fact I don't know you at all so don't go around putting words into girls mouths please!'

Of course he had gone too far. As if this mad experiment could ever work. Her answer led him back to the old world of which he was a lifelong inmate. Her answer scared him even though it had just jumped out of her. He wanted her to say that he had a nice smile or that she liked his eyes. To blame it on drink told him he was attractive only to dulled senses that would sharpen and scream. The band started and the pictures began to rattle. The singer was fat and thirty and looked as though she had seen and touched everything. Her skirt clung and her pointed heels twisted and ground into the wooden stage. But her deep, crooning voice swept through the hot fog like a great round human lighthouse that beamed out music rather than light to the room and beyond.

A little boy stood just behind the stage, next to a pram, his eyes wide open as he looked at the room swell and eddy before him, rising and falling and breaking against the stage. It was hard to say who was sinking and who was swimming.

By the big lighthouse, next to some pretty rocks, a lone figure stood gazing at the upstairs balcony. Jack looked down into the sparkling gloom and thought he knew who it was but as he was standing inert and silent, decided it couldn't be Gerry. Then he fell into another kiss in the hope that tonight had sprung from him alone and belonged to no-one else.

A Potted History of the World

by

Ali Batts

Mother Earth was, pissed! Boy was she pissed! All that effort and did anyone appreciate it - not bloody likely! Thousands of years she'd worked at it, bringing life and beauty to the surface of the planet, but did any of those ungrateful animals appreciate the care that went in to finding quite so many shades of green?

'I suppose they think it's easy,' Mother Earth muttered to herself, 'Look at them running about - frolicking and gambolling. Never mind that I'm utterly exhausted producing non stop sunsets and sunrises, making sure the sun shines when it's supposed to and raining on the right places. Do they care? Not at all! For all they care I may as well not be here at all.'

Mother Earth considered for a while, 'Everybody needs to be appreciated,' she thought to her self. 'What I should do is create an animal who can appreciate the art in what I do. Now, I don't want to start from scratch, so what animal could I use?'

Mother Earth thought for a time about some of the possibilities for 'enhancement'. After a few decades of serious consideration she came to the conclusion that, with a few minor adjustments, the apes would provide the ideal solution.

A few thousand years later Mother Earth decided that she had the definitive, art appreciating, animal. Admittedly it looked rather peculiar, having lost most of its hair over the years (except for patches in the oddest places) and okay so the males had these terribly unaesthetic dangly bits that tended to get in the way rather (especially when the animals were running) and occasionally got caught on twigs causing the poor things rather a lot of discomfort.

But the females though, well Mother Earth was well pleased with the females. They seemed to be rather intelligent and had ended up a lovely, round, soft shape.

Many of them seemed to be of quite an artistic temperament and they had taken to decorating the walls of the caves that they were living in with representations of some of Mother Earth's favourite animals.

Yes, all in all, Mother Earth was very satisfied. She was at last getting her due. The females had begun to celebrate the growing things that Mother Earth

45

Many of them seemed to be of quite an artistic temperament and they had taken to decorating the walls of the caves that they were living in with representations of some of Mother Earth's favourite animals.

Yes, all in all, Mother Earth was very satisfied. She was at last getting her due. The females had begun to celebrate the growing things that Mother Earth had provided for them, while the males sat around, obviously rather confused by all the activity.

What Mother Earth had forgotten (after all she did have an awful lot on her mind) was that with the exception of prodding the odd animal with a sharp stick to provide snacks for the group, the males had nothing much to do *except* sit around looking confused. In fact for a long, long time these two activities were just about the only things the males could do.

Until one day, a young male who was rather brighter than the others decided that sitting around with the other males and poking animals with sharp sticks was definitely not his idea of a fulfilling existence and besides, although he practised looking confused every day, he found he couldn't keep it up for more than a couple of hours at a time.

The young male tried his hand at what the females had come to call 'art' but was a miserable failure at it, much to the amusement of the females and, of course, confusion of the males.

He tried to produce a young one, stuffing himself with food until he was quite enormous and drinking himself stupid on the amazing drink the females made. Unfortunately this only had the effect of making him topple over rather frequently, when he had to be helped up by four or more of the females, again causing much mirth.

After many seasons had passed and there was still no sign of the hoped for birth, he came to the conclusion that he must be doing something wrong somewhere.

By this time the young male was fast approaching middle age, about twenty three or twenty four years old and was of course well past his prime.

He decided he had to work fast before it was too late and came to the conclusion that the only course of action was just to tell everyone that he was brilliant at everything.

Before long he had convinced the rest of the males that the females couldn't have produced young without his help, although he was always somewhat vague about the help he actually gave.

The females thought this was hilarious and spent long evenings having a good laugh and telling Mother Earth about it, (of course Mother Earth knew all

46

about it anyway, but she liked to keep in touch with her most interesting creations).

This was the beginning of the end, the long road downhill had started. In the blink of an eye, or so it seemed to Mother Earth, the tables were turned. Men had control over everything of importance and were even claiming that she was male. The cheek of it!

Well, Mother Earth sat down to think things over. This wasn't quite what she had planned. Even some of the women had started to forget about her. No, this wouldn't do at all.

Unfortunately it takes a deity so long to consider everything and plan everything that as far as I know she's still sitting.

Perhaps, with a bit of luck, she'll come to a conclusion soon.

Is Revenge Sweet

by

Wilhelmina Mackintosh

Lisa looked at the man sitting on the bar stool, the glass almost at her open mouth as she stared in disbelief. She slowly brought the glass to her lips and sipped the liquid which went down the wrong way making her cough.

When she stopped coughing she looked again at the face which was etched in her memory. The face that had haunted her over the past ten years and yet to make absolutely sure she went up to the bar and ordered another drink before letting her eyes wander in his direction.

He was watching her over his glass and there was the proof on the small finger of his hand, that unforgettable snake ring with the small ruby eye. He gave her a wink and she in return gave him a withering look that made him drop his eyes immediately. For a brief moment she had the urge to yell at him, to let out all the pent up feelings which had been festering within her for so long, instead she lifted her glass with an unsteady hand and returned to her seat.

Memories of that fateful day returned flooding back as clear as yesterday.

Lisa ran along by the river edge and being a happy, friendly teenager she stopped for a few minutes to ask the fisherman how many fish he had caught. After a brief conversation she continued on her way home taking the short cut through the small wooded area. She hadn't gone far when she heard a shout behind her and turning round saw the fisherman running towards her. At first she thought he might be giving her some of his catch but as he came closer she was filled with an uneasy fear and immediately turned to run. It was too late for within seconds he had pulled her to the ground. She struggled and fought but he succeeded in raping her then walked away unconcerned, leaving her weeping in terror among the trees.

It was the single tear that ran down her cheek and splashed into her glass that brought her back to the present and just in time to see the man leave the bar.

Without knowing why, she followed him outside keeping behind him at a safe distance. He continued down the street then turned left walking quickly

traffic followed him. She watched him head for a block of flats so she quickened her step reaching them as he entered the front door.

Lisa stood for a few seconds then decided to follow him in but just as she was about to enter several children came running out almost knocking her down. Putting out her arm she stopped the last one.

'Was that John Black that went in just as you kids were coming out?' she asked.

A freckled little face looked up at her.

'I'll tell you for fifty pence.' He told her cheekily.

She took the coin out of her bag and handed it to him. He looked at it in his hand and with a big smile said.

'No one called that name lives in the flats, Missus.'

Lisa was disappointed but only for a second for as the lad ran off he called.

'That was crabby George Wilson that went in.'

Lisa smiled, pleased that she had got the information she required. She pondered on her next move her brain going into overdrive and then she noticed the telephone kiosk across the road. That's it, she thought as she made her way through the traffic.

She hoped that he had a phone as she thumbed through the directory. Eventually she found his number and immediately dialled it with shaking hands and without any idea of what she was going to say.

Lisa hesitated when she heard his voice, then all the words that she had ever thought about him or called him over the years came flooding out of her mouth of their own accord and through her tirade she heard him ask.

'Who the hell are you?'

When she finally stopped speaking there was silence momentarily and then he spoke.

'I know who you are. You are that tart from Blackpool, well you got exactly what you deserved, you bitch.'

So I'm not the only one he raped, she thought angrily before saying quietly.

'George Wilson, every step you take I'll be behind you, watching your every move. Even at this moment I'm closer than you think, watching - waiting to pay you back.'

She could hear him yelling, 'Who are you? How do you know my name?'

Lisa put the phone down quietly and left the kiosk making her way slowly along the footpath and at the same time keeping her eye on the door of the flats. As she expected the door burst open and a very angry man came running out. He stopped briefly, his eyes darting this way and that looking at every fe-

out. He stopped briefly, his eyes darting this way and that looking at every female that passed by. His eyes then went to the kiosk which was occupied again and he headed for it straight out into the thick of the traffic. There was a screech of brakes, a dull thud and his body went flying up into the air landing yards away.

Lisa watched the crowd gather before crossing the road. She pushed her way through and looked at the crumpled body lying at her feet. His eyes were open, staring blindly, there was blood coming out of his mouth and ears. A man walked over to him and knelt down trying several places on the still body to find a pulse then he looked up and shook his head.

Lisa walked away. She neither felt pity nor pleasure at his death. Yes, this man had received what he deserved but this thought did nothing to alleviate the painful memories that had marred her young life.

Hughie's Hidden Talent

by

Joan Gaffney

In a dilapidated cottage near my childhood home lived Hughie, unmarried and alone. From out of a mat of night black hair crowned with a peaked cap, stuck a long thin nose in a shallow small face. No teeth, several coats over greasy black trousers were his winter and summer and night and day wear. Lots of people would give Hughie coats. If they hoped to tidy him they were disappointed. Hughie just put one coat on top of the other and wore the lot.

He had no possessions worth mentioning and if he cared we didn't notice. Hughie lent a hand on neighbouring farms. Any farmer wishing to employ him had to waken him and supply him with his breakfast. It was no mean feat to waken Hughie. Years ago his mattress had collapsed through the bed irons and Hughie being Hughie just stepped over and lay between on the floor. If he didn't want to work he remained out of sight in his den. Such foibles didn't raise an eyebrow in the country and certainly it didn't occur to us to offer to fix his bed for him.

Often when my father had succeeded in wakening and feeding him he'd slide quietly away to have a second breakfast elsewhere leaving my father to fume alone in his fields. It was useless to remonstrate with Hughie as he only retreated into some remote world. The trick was to stick close to him and escort him to the field.

'He's an inoffensive old soul,' said mother.

'He's not one damned bit soft,' said father.

Hunger was on Hughie at all times. When a fry was in preparation Hughie began rubbing his hands and sliding his tongue round his lips in anticipation.

'Would you like some more tea,' we'd ask.

'Aye some more tea to finish the bread,' he'd say.

Then you'd get a longing look from brown spaniel eyes and you'd say, 'Some more bread Hughie?'

'Aye. Some more bread to finish the tea.' The pantomime ended when we left him to finish alone.

Hughie was singularly uninformed about any religion. Above our fireplace hung a picture of Our Lord in the long robes of his time. Hughie studied the

51

picture for weeks and we studied Hughie studying the picture. At last he spoke, 'I never knew God was a woman,' said he.

My mother's hospitality extended to all the Hughies of this world even if the swankiest of visitors were expected. My patience was often stretched when I had to explain to my incredulous friends that no, Hughie was really no relation. We were never sure how much Hughie knew or understood. He never took part in conversations but a beatific smile came over his face when he sat ensconced by the fire in good company. The grease in his clothes began to melt and the smell that arose was well, just a Hughie smell. I can still recall vividly that smell.

If you asked him a question he'd look at you for a while. Then he'd answer in a rush as if he wanted to get it over and done with and hoped you wouldn't be asking any more questions.

'Is Jack Brown alive or dead?' asked my father.

A long pause.

'He is Tommy, aye,' said Hughie.

Hughie loved to be given a cigarette. He'd turn it in all directions and examine it well before he'd light it. Then he practically devoured it.

We all expected Hughie to finish his days in this pattern but we were in for a surprise. It all started very simply with our budgerigar. One day he slipped out of his cage and flew straight to Hughie. Now this my mother did take as a personal insult.

'Imagine that budgie going to the likes of Hughie,' she raved. But that wee budgie had been born for greater things. He'd left our house not being able to speak. He arrived back, a week later, talking.

Now the country side flocked to our house to see this miracle and to hear our budgie calling himself, 'Good wee Hughie.'

Hughie's fame spread far and wide. Everyone with a mute budgie descended on Hughie and anyone who hadn't one, bought one. Some owners cleaned his house. Some cleaned Hughie and lo and behold someone cut his hair. Food and cigarettes arrived in abundance and a box was found convenient to the door for those who wished to contribute. A line of gleaming cages hung from the ceiling and gleaming cars arrived to collect Hughie clone budgerigars.

No more farmwork for Hughie. He was now a full blown budgie elocutionist. His skills were in demand at fairs and bird clubs. As Hughie passed round the cigarettes I'd sometimes surprise a sly gleam in his eye.

'My father was right,' I'd think, 'You're not one damned bit soft.'

Oh Susannah

by

Marilyn Frazer

Susannah was a large and lazy lady. She wore an air of sleepy comfort and was not at all a noticing sort of person. She barely noticed where the children left their toys and dirty socks, or how the cat had kittens in the airing cupboard. She went easily through life.

She had weathered early widowhood with tea and buns, and was comfortably off. Her friends came often, always dropping in. Susannah never organised anything. She'd laugh and greet them, always pleased and never busy. She'd put the kettle on and get out sticky gooey things to eat she'd baked or bought. She did not discriminate. They'd clear a layer of cardigans and books from the armchairs in the big bay window and sit in the sun.

'Help yourself,' Susannah would say, and helping herself she'd kick off her shoes and draw her plump feet up under her. She'd admit with a sleepy smile that she had no news.

'But I don't mind,' she'd say. 'Tell me yours.' For she loved listening. She'd hear it all, without criticism or advice, and laugh at the funny bits. Nothing shocked her, nothing won condemnation from her. Her friends loved her. She was like a comfortable old chair, softly easing all aches and pains. Her friends had divorces and desperate love affairs, and brought Susannah their tales of pain and triumph. One friend once brought her brother, Ivor, an uneasy bachelor. He padded around in Susannah's wake and helped put out pastries on a plate. He said not much, but his eyes never left Susannah.

'Piggy little eyes,' Cissie said to Sarah, but that was behind everybody's back. He came again, alone, to mend Susannah's broken gate and walked her children and her dog. Susannah shrugged and said she didn't mind if it made him happy. She didn't mind when he sought to know her better. But he floundered on her perplexing indolence.

'I'd have to think about it.' She said, and shrugged. And while she thought - she took her time for everything - he kept on dropping around until they'd both got used to things being just as they were. Or at least Susannah did.

She got so used to him coming around that she barely noticed when he stopped.

53

'But where has Ivor been?' she asked.

'Spending time with Annabel. Annabel has designs on him. A shame. I thought one time that you and he -'

'Why, so did I,' said Susannah, pondering.

She found she noticed Ivor now by his absence, that somehow being more noticeable than his presence. He called to fix her gate again. He was a noticing sort of man, and driving by on his way to Annabel's had seen its reassumed droop.

Susannah greeted him with a new attentiveness, he noticed this and venturing his hand upon the softness of her shoulders, as they sat among the teacups and chocolate buns, he found himself rewarded with the cosy sugary kiss that he had pined for.

Annabel, being an extremely noticing sort of woman, soon perceived an absent-mindedness in Ivor and tracing his erring thoughts to Susannah's door, arrived there one day, all unexpected, her tap-tap-tapping at the door awakening Susannah from an armchair doze and disturbing the cats, who all sat up and pointed their ears. Susannah's usual callers just opened the door and came on in, so she knew this was no ordinary visitor and blinking away her sleepiness, buttoned the top buttons of her blouse over the bounty of her bosom and considered for a moment clearing the muddled ironing from the sofa, but the tap-tap-tapping grew more imperative.

'Ah Susannah,' Annabel said, when the door opened. 'If it had been anyone else, I'd have thought you were out, it took you so long to come to the door, but I know you never go anywhere.'

'So nice to see you Annabel. This is a surprise. You must take me as you find me.'

For even Susannah noticed Annabel eyeing the chaos of her home. Annabel had no time for Susannah. She considered her merely a slovenly person and feared it was somehow catching.

'My dear,' she said, 'How homely , and comfortable; but where will I sit?'

Susannah moved a washing basket from a chair and offered tea.

'No, no. I'm on a diet.' Annabel said, and sat down on the edge of a chair, flinching as a cat jumped in behind her.

'I haven't seen you for so long,' she said. 'I was wondering how you are, and really Susannah, I'm surprised to see you still haven't picked yourself up. How many years since Martin died? It must be five; its time you did something with your life. You're still a young woman. And there's no point shutting yourself away, closing out life. Look at me - I was shattered when Hugh left me - abso-

54

lutely shattered, but I didn't let myself go. I took control of my life - I've always been in control. My house is perfection, my garden impeccable, my appearance gets all my attention. I got out and about, did things, got a little job, built up my confidence. I'm in my prime Susannah, and I'm proud to say, I'm entirely a self-made woman. I've made my life be just as I want it. What I want I get - I don't mind saying it, I will say it again - I get what I want, be it job, first prize in flower arranging or man', to which last word she gave an ominous emphasis that went totally unnoticed by Susannah.

Annabel, quite sure she'd made herself clear, rose and glaring at the cat in the chair brushed hairs off her neatly pleated skirt. 'Well I won't keep you back from your ironing,' she said and left.

Susannah, making no connection, never asking why Annabel had called, quite missing the gauntlet that had been thrown down, pondered only some of Annabel's words. Was life passing her by? Was there more to be had that she'd somehow not noticed?

She joined a crochet circle. The gossip was good. She progressed to an occasional night out with her new friends. Someone suggested she try a night class - learn typing. It was fun. She lost weight, fell into a nice little job, and was not always in when Ivor dropped round, and he, at a loose end, married Annabel.

Susannah minded slightly. She was a little hurt, but she'd not miss him much.

'And he had such piggy little eyes,' Cissie said, this time to Susannah's face, 'And anyone careless enough to get himself married to Annabel deserves all he gets.'

Susannah laughed. She was a student now, her house was full of books and papers, the ironing still not done. Her friends called round to talk, and Susannah, more wakeful now, had news to share.

One day, months later, her garden gate fell off its hinges at her touch, and Susannah, late for a bus wondered for a moment what it was that the crooked gate reminded her of. Then she rushed on, and there was Ivor at the library. He did not recognise her, her hair was changed, then: 'Susannah! Well fancy meeting you! You do look well. Well, well, well -'

She smiled, not in her old slow way that he remembered.

'I have missed you,' he said, and then unguardedly, for she had always been so undemanding, unremarking that all around her had dropped guard. He said, not meaning to: 'Can I come back?'

Her regard was unrewarding.

'To see you,' he stumbled on, 'Some evening - I miss the way we used to be.'

But now he knew he had missed his mark, for Susannah, instead of laughing at him in her old lazy, careless way, was looking at him silently, guardedly.

'I didn't really mean to marry Annabel,' he said.

'But Ivor, dear,' Susannah spoke at last. 'It's much too late to mind or mend.' And then she left, the decisive tap-tap-tapping of her high heels crossing the library floor and disappearing through the door. And Ivor, uneasy husband, had to agree.

Uncle Enda

by

Paul MacCauley

My da has never liked Uncle Enda. He has always called him a good for nothing and a lazy loafer. But I love him. It seems strange, to me, to have to call him Uncle. After all he's only five years older than me. I've always felt that he's more like a big brother. I've no brothers and I'm saddled with the awful luck of having three sisters.

Uncle Enda lives in Monaghan. We usually go there for our holidays in July. We live in Belfast where relatives are pretty thin on the ground. In fact the only one I know is my da's Aunt Mary. She is fat and seems to spend most of her time minding other peoples business. I think she hates me. She's always slapping me round the head for not having my hair combed or something else like that.

I remember the day when Uncle Enda came to live in our house. He was, as they say, like a breath of fresh air, and of course the reason he came made it all that more exciting too. In fact, it was because of this that I rose in status in the eyes of the other lads in the neighbourhood. Uncle Enda plays soccer. We all knew he must've been good. Cliftonville had signed him up to play in the Irish League. Of course my da got a lot of mileage out of this. He went on about that it wasn't right for any self respecting Irishman to play soccer.

'It's a silly oul English game.' He said.

He thought that any sporting young fellah's ambitions should be either be swinging a hurley stick in Croke Park or to be kicking goals for Down against Kerry. Soccer is a dirty word in our house. I've been a secret Liverpool supporter for four years. That's all out in the open now and my da doesn't like it. He blames it all on Uncle Enda.

'And who's going to keep him?' He said to my ma. 'This Cliftonville team aren't going to pay a living wage. They're only part-timers and not too successful at that. I'm only a crane driver. I don't own the timber yard.'

'But he's my youngest brother. We can't let him roam the streets. This could be his opportunity to get into the big time. He might end up going across the water to one of those big teams.'

'Nonsense woman. He's a no hoper. He'll be turning the young lads head. He'll be giving him all sorts of daft notions.'

Despite all my da's ranting and raving my ma held a big party for Uncle Enda the night he arrived. She bought all sorts of sweets, buns, cake and Coke and Fanta too. It was all there. It was great. She got a video in for the occasion. My sisters were even in a good mood. I was allowed to bring my mates Stevie and Marty in. What a night it was. Of course my da fell asleep half way through the film.

The next day, after school, Uncle Enda took me, Stevie and Marty down to the park. He did goalkeeper and let us practise shooting in. It was great. He did a commentary, just like John Motson on Match of the Day. I was Brady, Stevie was Stapleton and Marty was O'Leary. We beat Spain four nil and, on the way home he bought us all ice cream in the Italian Ice Cream Parlour.

Then came the day of Uncle Enda's first game. It was at Ballymena. Of course my da wouldn't go near it. And anyway he was working overtime down at the timber yard.

'Someone's gotta bring some money into this house.' He said.

But anyway, Stevie's da was a Cliftonville fanatic. Never missed a match, home or away, rain, hail or snow, as they say. He said he'd take me and of course he was really busting to get talking to Uncle Enda. He liked that sort of thing, being all matey with the players and all. He had a word with my ma and she agreed. So we set off for Ballymena in his Ford Transit Van. Stevie sat in the front. Me and Marty sat in the back on big paint tins which we covered with cushions, to make the journey more comfortable.

The game was magic. Uncle Enda controlled the midfield. It was all Cliftonville. Ballymena held out until a minute before half-time. Uncle Enda made a fantastic run through the middle and had a crack at goal. The keeper didn't smell it. The ball hit the back of the net like a bullet. We all went daft, dancing and cheering, holding our red and white scarves above our heads.

'Brilliant! he's brilliant!' Shouted Stevies da.

I really felt proud. My uncle was a hero. The second half was a repeat of the first. Uncle Enda set up the second goal for the big centre forward who rose above the defence and nodded it into the net.

Stevie's da went mad.

'He's a cracker!' he shouted, 'Best I've seen in years.'

On the way home he took us into a chip shop and bought us all fish suppers and Coke. We ate them in the van then we headed home.

That night my da was in a real bad mood. There was a big write up, of the match, in Ireland's Saturday Night and the reporter named Uncle Enda man of the match. He even got a mention, in Sports Round Up, on the T.V.

He said to my ma. 'I don't see what all the fuss is about. He's not getting any readys for it. He'll have to get a real job. He can't live in a dream world all his life.'

The next Tuesday, Uncle Enda took me to his training session. We walked down the town and got the bus up to the ground. All the players made a fuss of me and the manager gave me a pound to buy sweets. On the way home we stopped off at the Italian Ice Cream Parlour.

My da gave off when we got home. 'He's to get up school in the morning you know. It's far too late. He should have been in bed ages ago.'

Uncle Enda said he was sorry and I didn't get to any more training sessions. But I got to all the Saturday matches thanks to Stevie's da.

Everything went well for two months. I enjoyed myself no end. It was brilliant. I was a hero at school. Then the news came that Uncle Enda would have to go away. I didn't know what to think. I was really happy for him but I knew life in our house would never be the same without him.

Of course my da, he was delighted. 'At last he's going. He's sponged off me long enough. I'll bet he doesn't remember to send me a few quid when he's making the big money over there.'

Uncle Enda had signed for Notts Forest. Stevie and Marty said that I might get to meet Brain Clough and this made me feel a bit better about the whole thing. Of course now I had to drop all the oul Liverpool connections. And Uncle Enda sent me a Forest scarf. That was only the start of it. After that came the strip and boots and a signed match ball. I was the envy of the neighbourhood.

And then it happened. The Big Match Live on Sunday. Forest V Arsenal at the City Ground. My ma let all my mates in to watch it in our house. And she got a video tape of my own so I could record it. My da sat on his chair and let on to doze. But I could see him, now and again, opening his eyes when Uncle Enda's name was mentioned.

It was one each and into the last five minutes of the match, when Uncle Enda took a dig from twenty yards. Just out of the blue, a real scorcher it was, into the top left hand corner. The players mobbed him and the crowd went daft. It even brought a half smile to Brain Clough's face. But my da got up and went upstairs.

Later in the week my ma got a letter and it was post marked Nottingham. We all knew who it was from. There was three pages of letter for her and two pages specially for me and a cheque for my ma for five hundred quid.

My da said. 'It's about time he starting paying me back. He ate us out of house and home for nearly three months.'

A few weeks later, to everybody's surprise, my da did a complete turn around and changed his attitude. It all started when Jack Charlton named Uncle Enda, in the Republic's squad, to play Spain in Dublin. We were baffled by this change of heart. He even wrote Uncle Enda a letter. We just couldn't understand it. Then he got a letter back from Nottingham. But he never showed us what was inside.

But my ma found out the next Saturday morning. She met Mister Lavery, who just happens to own the timber yard where my da works. When my ma got home it all come out in the open.

'Who's been licking round the boss?' she said.

My da's face went red.

'Got him tickets for the big match didn't you? I suppose you think you're the fellah in the big picture bumming and blowing about Enda.'

It was after this that my da conceded to take me to the big match. And ever since it's all been plain sailing. And I think there's a strong possibility that he's taking me to the World Cup Finals in Italy. My ma says he can well afford it seeing he's got promotion at work. I think Mister Lavery's going to Italy as well.

Piano Man

by

Ronan Blaney

The place was about fifty metres long and thirty metres wide. There were no windows and the only light came from a dim red bulb. This bare monotony was partially relieved by a piano which stood against the back-wall.

'How much do you want?' said Brian, our drummer.

The man looked at the rain pouring down outside. I'd disliked him immediately. His sharp tone of voice and his lean and watery face were characteristics I was too used to in places which appreciated nothing but well-rehearsed words and behaviour.

'Fifteen a week.'

Ducky, who was always better at these things than the rest of us, retorted.

'For a place with no heat and barely any light?'

He continued to stare out the door.

'Twelve then.'

'Ten then,' said Ducky.

That was it. The man handed Ducky the keys and told us to make sure we locked up when we left or

'Well... ' He'd waved his hands vaguely.

We set up the equipment.

'At least there's a socket,' murmured Paul.

'I like it,' said Brian, 'it has a feel about it.'

The rest of them nodded. I didn't. Aside from my reservations about the cold and the dimness, there was something unnerving about its pristine vacancy and its one anomaly. Constantly throughout the rehearsal my eyes kept returning to the piano which hid among the shadows of the far wall. Because that was the thing. It did seem to hide. No one mentioned it, no-one even seemed to notice it.

The rehearsal went well however. Better than well even. The acoustics of the place seemed exceptionally good. The guitars sounded sharp and pure, the vocals didn't disappear in the noise and, for once, the tone and rhythm of the bass and drums sounded like music rather than a series of erratic and dull thuds. We even got a new song together. This was the first one we'd written in what

61

seemed like ages. The truth of the matter was that the group was gradually breaking up. Most of us had neither the time nor the energy anymore.

'Thinking Man's Jingly-Jangley' had been formed on a whim. After a bout of festive drunkenness Ducky had asked Brian and myself to bring our guitars up to his attic. We discovered that we did know a few common tunes and that an almost insanely embarrassed Paul could sing. Every Saturday after that and the odd few Sundays for the next two years we would practice. Our enthusiasm was boundless. Neither a guitar with strings missing, a bric-a-brac drum-kit, or a microphone that switched off when it was moved violently, stopped us from antagonizing neighbours or kin. And after each practice-session we would re-play the tapes which had been recording during this sincere and tormented chaos and try to find something of merit. Then it was a fast trot towards the pub to discuss the exigencies of world domination:

'I don't think we should do interviews y'know,'

'And no back-stage parties either I hate all of this oh-aren't-we-all-so-successful crap.'

'I'd still live in Ireland, in the North.'

'Imagine never having to say 'Yes sir, No sir to anybody.'

The rest of these weeks were a series of clannish conspiracies in classrooms, and eager anticipations of each others' new chord progressions and rhythms.

Things had changed however. The only new ideas I heard were my own and I even felt forced to demonstrate these with an air of self-defensive indifference. Rehearsals sometimes never went ahead - someone either had a job to go to or a girl to see - and when they did, three times out of four, they would break up after an hour or so. This lock-up was a last-ditch attempt to retrieve something.

'We can go there when we want to,' I had said. 'We can bring down a few beers, play away, and have a bit of crack. Get away from it all.' To my surprise they all agreed.

'That wasn't bad at all,' said Paul as he was turning off the lights. 'This place will do.'

I nodded, but the satisfaction I felt was wrapped up - tinged or tainted - by something else which I could not define. As the meagre red light went out my mind was involuntarily drawn to the back of the lock-up. Its occupant had somehow become more and more animate to my imagination as the rehearsal had gone on. Suddenly, I pictured myself running my hands over the piano's mahogany flanks.

We went to the pub afterwards. Ducky's and Brian's girlfriends' were there. They discussed politics and food, I played the slot-machine. When I came back to the table I was admitted into the conversation.

'That was a good song you wrote,' Brian began.

'We wrote,' I said.

Brian laughed.

'You're improving with age,' he finished.

While walking home I asked Paul what he thought of the piano.

'What piano?' He answered.

'The one... forget it,' I said.

I never slept that night.

I went to see the owner of the lock-up the next day.

'I want you to get rid of it,' I commanded.

He sat in silence for perhaps thirty seconds as if composing himself. Eventually he said, 'You move it.'

Why doesn't he ask why? I thought. Only later did it occur to me that he had not even asked what 'it' was.

'It's your place, not mine. We're paying... '

'I don't want to look at the thing,' he cut in, and for the first time looked me in the face.

He was looking for the question just as much as I was so I broke the deadlock.

'Why?' I said.

'It was my son's.'

'And?'

'He's dead now. Slashed his wrists.'

The man's bluntness shocked me.

'I'm sorry,' I stammered, not sure whether to proceed or not.

He wanted to talk however.

'He played that thing all the time. Played it well too. Sometimes I thought that everything that was good and beautiful in him came out on that box. He never talked y'see.'

The candidness of a stranger can be moving.

'Why move it out there then?' I said softly.

His voice took on a new angrier tone.

'Because he was a selfish lie.' He stopped momentarily. yet in this moment my interest waned. It was only with a mild curiosity that I now regarded him and his words.

'My wife died two months after him, she never got over it. He wasn't worth it and that thing,' he couldn't even give it a name, 'hid his poison,' his hands shook, 'his emptiness.'

I dreamt that night.

The lock-up seemed as spacious as a football stadium yet as lifeless and silent as a morgue. I walked towards the far end unperturbed by the grotesque shadows which leapt against its back wall. Like some sort of up-ended spider he lay sprawled over the piano with his arms and legs waving madly. He had an effete, almost girlish face, and rank, blackish-red blood poured from him. I turned in disgust. For a period of what seemed like immeasurable time I stood and stared. My guitar lay on the ground before me.

Yet the piano stayed and we practiced on.

The dream still recurs. It never varies but, by now, its portents mean less to me than a handful of rotting dust. Why? It is because I still dislike the man and understand the boy.

The Bogey Club

by

Charlotte Macauley

'I've met some eejits in my day, but you have to be the biggest one of all Tommy Brennan.' Why can't you be like other men and take up darts or football as a hobby?' A red-haired girl in her late twenties attacked the shirt on the ironing board with great ferocity.

'I don't know why you're going on at such a rate. I'm not the only one in the club after all.' Tommy eased himself out of the armchair by the fire and lifted a packet of cigarettes from the mantelpiece.

'You don't catch big James's sister yapping at him all the time.' He pushed a cigarette into the side of his mouth.

'Och! sure you know why Sheila McMeekan doesn't give off to him don't you? She's only too glad to get rid of him so she and Davy Donelly can have the house to themselves.'

Mary pulled the shirt onto a coat hanger and hung it over a chair. She was a good looking girl with a well proportioned figure. 'Well stacked' is how Tommy's mates described her.

'I think it's ridiculous a group of grown men meeting every week to watch Humphrey Bogart films.'

'It's not just his films we watch.' Tommy defended himself.

'Oh! sorry, I forgot. You all dress up like him as well. God in Heaven what must people think when they see you all coming up the Newtownards road together.' The vision of her brother and the other Bogart clones was enough to make Mary burst into laughter.

Tommy stubbed his cigarette out on the ashtray. 'I'm fed up with your wise cracks. I'm away round to the Welders for a drink.'

'It's a wonder they haven't nick-named you down in the shipyard yet.' She called after him. 'Phillip Marlow would be a good one, would suit you down to the ground in that get up of yours.'

Tommy slammed the door behind him. He was getting tired of people poking fun at him from all angles. Little did Mary know how right she was. For the past six weeks he'd become known as 'Marlow' down in the 'Yard'. At first, he'd been amused at his new title. But now the joke had ceased to be funny. Of

65

course he hadn't said anything to her about his nick-name. She would have had a field day at his expense.

As he walked up Dee street he spotted an empty Pepsi can by the kerb, and took out his anger on it by kicking it further up the street. He couldn't see what all the fuss was about. Sure look at the way Elvis fans behaved. Paying homage to him year in year out by trips to Graceland. Nobody seemed to think there was anything wrong with that. So what was so wrong about the Bogey club? maybe it did seem a bit odd them dressing up like their idol. But where was the harm in it?

Mary was in the process of painting her nails when Tommy came back from the Welders.

'Shouldn't you be getting changed?' She asked him, looking at her watch. 'James will be calling for you shortly.'

'Och! I'm fed up. I think I'll give the club a miss tonight.' He took off his coat and threw it over the settee.

'You'll do no such thing! Kathy is coming round to do my hair and I don't want you clocking under our feet.' Mary lifted the coat from the settee and threw it to her brother. 'Do you think I've nothing better to do than clear up after you? Now hurry up and get ready. I don't want that James McMeekan trying to chat Kathy up. You know how shy she is.'

Tommy had taken a cigarette from his packet and was about to light up. But the look on his sister's face, as she pointed to the freshly cleaned ashtray, put him off.

Mary's friend Kathy arrived a few minutes before Tommy left for the club. She was a pretty girl with shoulder length blond hair.

'Come on in Kathy. Mary will be down in a minute. She's washing her hair.' He tried his best to make her feel at ease. 'Give me your coat and sit down there by the fire.' He pointed to what he and Mary considered to be the best seat in the house. Tommy had never been particularly good with the opposite sex. But this girl was in a class of her own when it came to shyness, which only made matters worse. He reached into his pocket for his cigarettes. There was nothing like a smoke to calm the nerves.

'Would you like one?'

'No thank you Tommy. I don't smoke.'

'Oh! sorry I forgot.'

'It's not that I've anything against them. Its just that they make me cough. But you go ahead and have one yourself.' He hadn't noticed it before but she had the most amazing green eyes. Just then, a car horn hooted, much to his annoyance.

'Listen Kathy, I have to rush off now. But I'll see you again.'

'Okay Tommy I'll see you.'

'Conflict' was the film chosen by the club members tonight. They all huddled round the screen and watched Bogey try to win the hand of the gorgeous Alexis Smith. And when Sydney Greenstreet confronted their hero with the murder of his wife, everyone booed and jeered. But, nevertheless, it was agreed that it was a great film. The next hour was passed by exchanging tit bits of information gathered on the great man. Tommy was delighted with himself when it was his turn to speak.

'Did you know that 'Bogey' was so taken with Leslie Howard when he appeared with him in 'High Seirra' that he and Lauren Becal decided to call their daughter after him.' At the mention of High Seirra the others chipped in with recollections of the film. And so, it was, unanimously, decided that it should be shown the following week.

Kathy was still there when he arrived home.

'You're back early. What's wrong did you's run out of Humphry Bogart films?' Mary teased him, then, thinking the better of it, offered to make him some tea.

'Did you have a good night Tommy?' Kathy asked him when his sister disappeared into the kitchen.

'It was great. We saw a film called Conflict. Bogey fancied his wife's sister, so he bumps of his wife so he can marry the sister.' Tommy's face beamed with enthusiasm.

'Well did he?'

'Did he what?'

'Did he marry the sister?' She searched his eyes for an answer.

'No. Sydney Greenstreet saw to that.' He told her slowly, taking in every feature of her face. He hadn't realized just how pretty she was until now.

Mary returned with a plate of sandwiches and placed them on the coffee table. She looked at Kathy then her brother. 'Have I interrupted something?'

'Don't be daft!' Tommy's face reddened. 'I was just telling Kathy about the film we watched tonight.'

Kathy looked up at the clock on the wall. 'Oh! goodness, look at the time. I'll have to go Mary.'

Tommy wished that she didn't drive so that he would have the excuse of walking her to the bust stop. He wanted to ask her for a date but hadn't a clue how to go about it.

'Well I'll see you Tommy.' She took her time putting on her coat. He watched the car drive out of sight. He could have kicked himself. It wouldn't be long before a good looking girl like Kathy would be snapped up, and he had just passed up a great opportunity of asking her out.

'I don't believe it Tommy Brennan.' Mary shook her head. 'You're actually interested in someone. I thought you'd have to be sporting a hat and a trench coat to get your attention.'

The following Wednesday night Tommy was getting ready to go to the club as usual. He wondered why Mary was spending a lot more time on herself tonight.

'Are you going out or something?' He asked her.

'Yes I've a date. How do I look?' She flicked back her hair and pouted her mouth in an exaggerated way.

'You look great. But what about Kathy? Isn't it usually a Wednesday night she comes round?'

'Oh! Kathy has a date herself.'

Tommy's face dropped. He knew he should have made a move sooner. The doorbell rung and Mary let the visitor in. Tommy was surprised when he heard Kathy's voice.

'Why are you all dressed up?' She asked Mary. 'Are we going out somewhere?'

'No, I'm going out. You two are staying in.' She winked at Tommy. 'I thought somebody would have to do something about you pair. It was obvious that neither of you would ever make a move. There's a bottle of wine and lasagne in the fridge. Have a nice time! By the way, I've told James so you won't be disturbed. See you later then.'

Tommy watched Kathy's face for her response, and was relieved to see that she was as pleased as he was at his sister's matchmaking.

'She's not as stupid as she looks, is she?'

Kathy nodded her head in agreement.

'You make yourself comfortable. I'll get a couple of glasses.' He poured the wine slowly still not believing his good luck.

'I hope you don't mind missing the club because of me Tommy.'

'Not in the slightest.' He reassured her.

And when they tipped their glasses together, he knew Bogey would have been proud of him when he told her, 'Here's looking at you kid!'

Frank Lynn's Tale

by

Andrew Hammond

Based on an original story by Geoffrey Chaucer, with additional material by Charles Dickens. Apologies to both.

Hugh Squire stared at the fire. Frank Lynn shifted uneasily. He felt uncomfortable with the silence.

'When are you moving house?' said Frank.

'When am I moving house?' rejoined Hugh, 'Don't fucking talk to me! I'm not moving.'

'But I thought everything was agreed!'

'It was. We agreed weeks ago, then I heard this afternoon that the bastard sold it to someone else.'

'That's rough. Had you signed the contract?'

'No. He gave me his word! I thought that meant something, but he broke it for the sake of a few hundred pounds. Money! that's all that matters nowadays. The ethos of possessive individualism has created a selfish, money-grabbing society. Is there no decency left? Once your word was your bond, but that concept is as dead as the Age of Chivalry.'

Frank Lynn interrupted Squire, 'I sympathise, but don't lose heart. There are enough people to restore your faith in human nature. Let me recount a story I heard recently.'

Jeff was a computer-games designer with the leisure giant, Mega. He worked hard and achieved success when his game, *Arveragus the Noble Knight*, became the company's most successful product and a world-wide cult hit. He married his girl-friend, Bianca, who was one of the most beautiful women in the world, and to whom he was completely devoted. They lived in perfect bliss and happiness, until Jeff was sent to Japan to work on *Arveragus and the Black Rocks*, the successor to the cult game. Bianca was broken-hearted and began to drink heavily. Her friends, noticing her bacchanalian propensities, tried to cheer her up and moderate her drinking habits. Initially Bianca claimed she was too depressed and stayed at home to read and re-read Jeff's letters from Japan.

Eventually she realised that going out would do her good. They went to a club, 'Dark Fantasy,' where the band, Rokkes Blake, were playing. This turned out to be an error in judgement. Bianca's friends had overlooked the fact Rokkes Blake was old English for Black Rocks. When Bianca saw the band she was so distraught she could hardly stand. She began mumbling incoherently.

'But, Lord, thise grisly feendly rokkes blake,
That semen rather a foul confusion
Of werk than any fair creacion
Of swich a parfit wys God and a stable,
Why han ye wrought this werk unresonable?'

Her friends thought, 'Oh no, she's drunk again!' and that her mind had finally gone. They ignored her and continued listening to the band. The singer was a friend of theirs, called Mick Jugular because the band played music in the same vain as the Rolling Stones.

Mick had loved Bianca for years, but never dared tell her this. He had fallen into despair and written many songs of unrequited love, but finally he plucked up the courage to declare his love.

'I love you, and for years have thought only of you. I know my devotion is in vain, and that my only reward has been a broken heart, but pity my sorrow, for with a word you can kill me or save me. I would die here at your feet! Do you fancy going out for a drink?'

Bianca looked at him. 'Wow! Heavy! You're a game boy to tell me this! But I can't be untrue to Jeff, in word or deed as long as I have sanity.' Then she jested, 'I'll be your lover, since you complain so piteously, if you get rid of all the *Black Rocks* computer games in the world so that people can talk to each other again.' Thanne wol I love yow best of any man, have heer my trouthe, in al that evere I kan.'

'But that's impossible! then must I die a horrible death!' Soon Mick was left alone in 'Dark Fantasy,' his mind deranged.

He prayed.

'Apollo, cast your merciful eye upon wretched Mick! Ask your sister, Lucina, the moon-godess, to make all those mad enough to have bought *Black Rocks* computer games even madder so that they will throw them away, or any others that they see, and organise industrial madness so that there will be a world-wide strike in the factories, or introduce a virus into the game. Then I can say to Bianca, 'Keep your promise, the Black Rocks have gone.' Apollo, do this

71

miracle for me. See the tears on my cheeks. Have compassion on me.' And with that he fainted.

His brother found him and took him home where he languished, in sickness and mental torment, for two years. When Mick recovered he went to Jamaica to spend a few weeks with his friend, Bob. Bob was a drugs dealer, and might know of a hallucinogenic drug that would lead people to believe that something no longer existed. Mick arrived at Bob's house a few days before Christmas and told him the story thus far. Bob knew of such a drug. They needed some B.R.D.D. (from the Latin - Blackus Rockus Disappearum Drugius), known colloquially as 'Rocks Off' and similar in effect to L.S.D. Their contact was known as Tiny Tim. They met him at a special Christmas Eve concert by Jacob Marley and the Wailers. Tiny Tim dropped some tabs, and on the subsequent trip an arcane figure warned Mick that three ghosts would visit him during the night - the ghosts of Love Past, Love Present and Love Future.

'What the Dickens!' exclaimed Mick.

The effects of the drug, however, wore off before any of the said ghosts appeared. These side-effects notwithstanding the drug seemed to work. There wasn't one *Black Rocks* game in sight! They returned to Bob's house to negotiate a price for the drugs and for smuggling them back to England. They agreed on one thousand pounds, but no money changed hands. Mick's word was enough.

'Ye shal be payed trewely, by my trouthe!'

Mick returned from Jamaica and at the earliest opportunity slipped Bianca some 'Rocks Off' tabs. He told her that he loved her and that she had pledged her trouthe to love him if he got rid of all *Black Rocks* games. It had been done. Her first reaction was one of relief, then horror as she realised the consequences. Bianca was dumb-founded. How could this be? It was a monstrous outrage, totally against the process of nature. She returned home and there was a wailing and gnashing of teeth. What should she do? To break her word would bring dishonour. To keep it would bring shame. Should she kill herself to remain loyal to Jeff? There seemed no escape, save death or dishonour. An unenviable choice, and one she faced alone for two days as Jeff was at a week-end seminar on the *Black Rocks II* game. When he returned home he asked what was wrong. Tearfully, Bianca told Jeff what had happened. He didn't understand. If she was having an affair he would rather hear the truth than some feeble excuse about Black Rocks.

'But,' he said, 'I don't want anyone saying we broke our word. Trouthe is the hyest thing that man may kepe.' He began to cry and told her to get out.

Bianca took another tab, and headed down to 'Dark Fantasy' where Mick's new band, The Magic of Illusion, were playing. She spoke to him, garbling about Black Rocks and promises. Mick looked at her.

'Oh god! You're completed wasted! I couldn't stand it if you'll be constantly stoned. I love you, but I'll not come between you and Jeff. In view of his noble behaviour, I release you from your trouthe.'

Bianca returned home and properly explained what had happened. Jeff forgave her and they lived happily ever after.

Mick on the other hand, had the problems of owing one thousand pounds to Bob and having a large supply of drugs with a very limited market. After his illness, and having just formed a new band, he was somewhat impecunious. He was unable to sell any of the tabs. Bob was now in London, so Mick called round, smoked a few joints and they went to the pub, 'Gentillese', where he explained the situation and assured Bob he would be paid.

Bob was touched by these noble acts, and said, 'If a computer programmer and a musician can be honourable, then so can a drugs-dealer. Sire, I releese thee thy thousand pound. I wol nat taken a peny of thee.'

They stayed until closing time, got drunk and on their way home were arrested for 'threatening behaviour.' Their case made the national press. The Tabloids carried 'Shock, Horror Probes.' The Quality Papers posed the question, 'Who was the most noble?' What do you think I can say no more, Frank Lynn's tale is at an end.

The Silver Sixpence

by

Edna Perrott

My innocent request to Mammy had a dramatic effect. She stood stock-still until I feared that like Lot's wife, she had turned into a pillar of salt, I was particularly partial to bible stories. I had only said, 'Mammy, now that I'm five, can we get a new baby?'

She still remained, rooted. Fear knotted my stomach. What had I done wrong this time? Long seconds passed before I heard Mammy clear her throat, a sure sign that she was angry.

'Now listen to me missy, the answer is No. I was forty-six when you were born and the laughing-stock of the street. Is nine of a family not big enough for you? You're not exactly starved for company. Sure your brother Willy's wee son is only four and you see him often enough.' I hung my head. It wasn't the same as having a new baby of your very own.

Mammy's voice brightened. 'And aren't you the only child in the street who was an aunt at six months old?'

I wished she hadn't reminded me but then she didn't know my awful secret - I hated being an aunt. Mammy and Daddy like me, had been the youngest in their respective families so all my aunts were old. They each had their own day for visiting and when they left, their own particular odour hung in the air like invisible fog.

'Holy God', Daddy would say when he arrived home from the shipyard, 'Was your Martha here the day? The place reeks of Sloan's liniment.' Martha was crippled with rheumatics.

Aunt Jane came infrequently. She suffered from 'A woman's complaint' and smelt strongly of ammonia. Mammy kept a rexine covered cushion which was placed hastily on the good chair when Aunt Jane arrived unexpectedly. When she left Mammy polished the cushion with Mansion polish. When I enquired abut the smell Mammy snapped, 'Mind your own business.'

My brother Stanley who was nine and next to me in age said it smelt of 'Pee.'

Mammy's sister Lucy was the only one of the lot I even liked. Daddy described her as 'a great tank of a woman'. She was harnessed into Spirella corsets which forced her ample chest up and outwards to such a degree that it

74

sat horizontally and she used it, covered by a hanky, on which to steady her cup and saucer. Every time she raised her fleshy arm to lift her cup I watched fascinated, the widening crescent of sweat staining her dress at the armpit. The tea finished she said, 'I'm just tortured with these flushes', and proceeded to pull her dress away from her neck, blow down the steep cleavage between her breasts and wipe between them with the hanky.

But it was Daddy's eldest sister, Aunt Ida, who terrified me. She was tall, thin and dressed entirely in black. Stanley said he thought she was a witch. Round her neck was a broad jet-beaded band, the skin left exposed wrinkled and reddish purple like the necks of the turkeys dangling head down in butchers' windows at Christmas. There were odd shaped brown blotches on her hands and, coarse dark hairs sprouted vigourously from moles on her chin. She expected to be kissed and they jagged like bristles of a scrubbing brush. When she bent to kiss me she exuded an odour of mothballs and decay.

One afternoon while she slept in her chair, 'full to the tonsils' after her dinner, she snored and her top denture slipped down, to hang grotesquely, exposing her empty gums. The sight of these monstrosities, white as our delph cups and edged in bubble-gum pink, scared the life out of me. Was this what Aunts turned out like? To reassure myself I felt my own top teeth to check their security and gave a tug at the front one. The tooth came away in my hand! My screams brought Mammy rushing from the scullery and wakened Aunt Ida.

'My teeth are falling out like hers,' I sobbed, big hot tears splashing down my cheeks onto Mammy's hands as she examined the gap.

Mammy's fright turned to embarrassment, 'She's not usually a fusser', she explained to Aunt Ida, thinking I was crying in pain. 'Give her here to me', she said taking me struggling and reluctant onto her boney lap and rocking me like a baby.

'You put that lovely wee tooth under your pillow to-night and the tooth fairy might exchange it for a piece of Silver.'

Between great gulping sobs I asked, 'What does she want it for?'

'To use as a lucky charm,' and then to Mammy, 'I should get the fairy to collect all this one's wee teeth and make me a set that fits.' They both laughed and were amazed at my renewed sobbing.

Mummy, in shame said, 'A big girl of five getting on like a cry baby.'

Aunt Ida, on leaving, said to Mammy in the hall, 'Don't be too hard on her, sure you know she 'takes after' me, she's highly strung. Put this under her pillow to-night,' and I heard the snap of her closing purse.

75

That night I prayed fervently 'Please God, don't let Aunt Ida take my teeth and don't let me 'take after' her.' To be on the safe side I hid my tooth in the Bourneville cocoa tin in which I kept my treasures but slept fitfully and wakened early and looked fearfully under my pillow. There it lay mocking me, a shiny, silver sixpence! So Aunt Ida was a witch. I rushed to the tin but my tooth was still there. The rumpus wakened Stanley, in the corner bed and I blurted out my story.

'Your teeth will grow again,' he said, 'Mine fell out and grew again, look.' And he opened his mouth wide. I was inconsolable.

'But she wants My teeth and you don't 'take after' her and you're not an aunt and you said yourself she looked like a witch.' Then I held out the shiny sixpence and watched Stanley's face lose it's confidence.

'I never got a whole sixpence for all my teeth put together,' he said and most frightening of all, he refused to take the sixpence when I offered to give it to him.

Over the months and years I lost many teeth and put them quickly into the kitchen range and told Mammy, 'big girls didn't believe in fairies.'

'So you're getting sense at last,' she said, relieved. But the dread of Aunt Ida never left me. When she came on Wednesdays I kept out of the house.

Mammy chided me, 'You were your Aunt Ida's favourite, and now you haven't a word to say to her. I just don't understand you at times.'

As time passed my second teeth became well established but my dislike of my aunt seemed deeply rooted.

I was ten when Aunt Ida was found dead in her kitchen. Mammy took us to pay our respects. Snapshots of her were passed round showing her at different stages of childhood. She looked remarkably like me. Mammy made me accompany her into the parlour where the body was laid out. She looked different in death, almost young.

'It's a great pity you were not close to her,' Mammy said, 'You two were so alike in nature and everything. She had a hard life bringing up your Daddy and his brother and two sisters. Your granny died young. She was too old to marry by the time the rest were reared and she really loved children. When I was so ill after you were born it was Ida who came and walked the floor with you every night for weeks. You were such a puny, wee scrap of a baby I sometimes think only she could have willed you to live.' Mammy took my hand saying, 'I want you to touch her, you owe her that much. Remember the dead can't hurt you - only the living do that,' Aunt Ida's forehead felt marble cold, 'In future,' Mammy continued 'Don't judge the book by the cover.'

That night guilt ate into my ten year old soul like acid. The sky was streaked with morning pink before I got things straight in my head. I still didn't feel any love for Aunt Ida but I knew now why I hated being an Aunt. Just as Mammy had felt a laughing-stock at having a baby when she was too old, I felt 'different' to other children for being an Aunt, too young. It was feeling 'different' that created the fear. I held the silver sixpence in my hand, George V's head on one side, 1934 dated on the other, the year I lost my first tooth.

I re-wrapped it in it's cushion of tissue paper and returned it to the cocoa tin. I knew with certainty I'd never part with it.

At the funeral I listened to all the good things people said about Aunt Ida. Maybe I'd improve as I got older. Sure, out of all the nine of us, wasn't I the only one who 'took after' her?

The River

by

Roy Kelso

A movement on the river bank caught the fisherman's eye. Pausing in his cast, he lifted his gaze from the slow moving waters of the Ballinderry with impatience. Look as he might though, the banks on either side were empty of life - save that of the gentle beckoning of the tall reeds, and the whispering leaves of hazel bushes which clung tentatively to the water-logged footings.

His concentration broken, he reeled in the Mayfly and waded to the bank. His sudden, noisy movements startling black waterhens which beat the water furiously with half-grown wings in their panic to reach the safety of the reeds. Sticklebacks darted in shoals as one out of the path of his waders, and the whirr of dragonflies filled the air. Flying into the rays of the sun with a dash of irradiant turquoise lest they too end up frozen forever in colour and flight around the band of the fisherman's paddy-hat.

Changing the tackle, he put a blackhead worm on the weighted line, cast out, then rested the rod on a forked stick. Opening his bag he took out his lunch and bit deep into a cheese sandwich, giving the tip of the rod a cursory glance now and then, his mind elsewhere. He knew the fishing was really a waste of time now. Not like the old days when the Ballinderry rushed and gurgled its way to distant Lough Neagh. Swollen by the tributaries of Slieve Gallion mountain.

Gone was the wonderful sight of a speckled trout leaping for flies and pure joy out of the peat-coloured waters. Gone too were the grey herons and the kingfisher. Their food source a thing of the past. Now it was a slow moving thing. Slurry and pesticides smothering the life in it, so that its movement through the wooded stretch of Tullagh was like that of an old man.

No, his annual visit to the river had become more of a pilgrimage. He knew his bag would return empty. No longer to contain the plump half-pounders, their rainbow colours wrapped in green grasses to keep them cool. It was more the memories of his childhood days which kept calling him back.

Marty smiled. Remembering the dire warnings of his Grandmother that the Ballinderry claimed a child every seven years. Unheedful of her fears, his pals and he spent every single day of those seemingly long, hot summers by the river. Fishing with make-shift rods whittled from hazel branches, their inces-

78

sant chatter and whoops of joy echoing through the tall trees. Or squatting in laurel-branch dens where potatoes were roasted on smoking fires. And on other days their patient and un-rewarding stalking of the grey heron with home-made bows and arrows.

Theirs was a time of freedom and laughter. Where the only richness which mattered was the warm rays of the sun stretching skinny frames, or brightening their hand-me-down wartime clothing. Their expectations were small. Only that those days would never end; and fear was an unknown quantity. So perhaps that is why, despite a Grannie's warning they flirted with that river unashamedly. Flying like trapeze artists over its dangerous depths on long ropes tied to over-hanging branches. Or shooting its rapids on flimsy rafts.

Yet no child would fall victim to its dull depths now. Like a silenced Loreli its song was muted, for no longer did the children's laughter echo around the woods, or at their old bathing place further along the bank. All that was left was a deep, sad stillness, and the remembered legend.

Marty's reverie was interrupted by a rustle in the tow-path behind him. He turned quickly in time to see a small spaniel dog rushing towards him, its tail wagging furiously. He immediately regretted throwing his crusts into the river as he held out his hand to pat it on the head. Sniffing inquisitively at his waders, it quickly lost interest and darted into nearby bushes.

'Pepe, Pepe!' A female voice called, her voice growing more strident. 'Where are you, you rascal... ?'

He smiled at the name. None of your Tobies or Spots now, he allowed to himself. Just then the caller came rushing up to the river bank, her face flushed with the chase. She gave a start when she saw him sitting there, then quickly regained her composure.

'Have you seen my dog anywhere?' She asked a little breathlessly.

The fisherman touched his hat carelessly, grinned, and replied, 'Aye Susan, it's away into the bushes there... '

The woman looked at him more closely when she heard him address her by name, then exclaimed, 'For God's sake is it yourself, Marty? It simply must be years... '

'Aye, it's a brave while now. You were still at the Technical when I left these parts,' Marty replied thoughtful.

'So what brings you back,' she enquired 'Sure everyone knows the fishing's been bad for donkey's years,' she went on, looking askance at the rod.

Marty gave a wry grin, suddenly embarrassed by the question.

'Och, I don't know. I kid the wife I make the long drive down here every year for the trout, but I suppose there's more to it than that. I can't seem to be able to get this place and its memories out of my system. Something always calls me back, and it's not for what I catch.'

Giving a cursory look around for her dog, Susan pulled off her mac and sat down beside him. Taking out a pack of cigarettes from the pocket of her jeans she offered him one. He refused, but watched her with interest as she lit up, took a deep drag, and then exhaled the smoke. Her eyes following the cloud as it drifted over the river. She sat smoking quietly for a time before going on.

'I still live over the hill,' she volunteered, nodding in the general direction of the Housing Estate where they'd all grown up. Hesitantly, as if carefully picking her words, she continued. 'I have never lost my love for this place either...' then suddenly blushed as she felt Marty's eyes meet hers.

Turning his head quickly to where the fishing line disappeared, taut like an anchor chain into the depths of the river, he asked, 'Do you ever see any of the old gang at all, Susan?'

'Oh aye. The most of them still live here in the town. Too slow to make the move to get away, not like you. All married with kids of their own. I don't expect they even remember about this place,' she allowed.

'I see Geordie - and what did you call that girl with the jampot glasses - down in the City an odd time,' Marty said as if anxious to show that he hadn't lost total contact with her world.

Susan thought for a moment, then her eyes lit up and she laid her hand on his arm. 'Myrtle! Remember we used to call her Myrtle the Cow?' They both laughed at the memory.

As if that first laugh was the key they launched into joyful reminiscing of their childhood days in Tullagh. Each vying with the other to put forward their particular recollection. Bringing back to life the quiet wood and sluggish river, if only for a while. The years falling away from their eyes and their faces alive with talk.

Tiring of its freedom, Susan's spaniel came creeping guiltily back to where they were sitting. It made to leap on her lap but she playfully pushed it away, admonishing it for the state of its coat. She rose then, her excuse for lingering gone, and said, 'I suppose I'd better be getting back now to fix Johnny and the boys their tea...'

Marty got to his feet also and helped her on with her Mac. Again the silence crept between them, suddenly shy now that the moment had come to part. Marty gave a forced laugh.

'Well, Susan, at least we have survived to prove my Grannie wrong. Sure the ould river must be starved for children.'

Susan turned to face him and gently touched his face.

'Perhaps we did Marty, but you remember the day she caught you and I in the laurel hut. What age were we then, fifteen? That year had to be a special one for the river for it claimed the innocence of two children, instead of one. That's why it will never let us go... '

Marty sighed. 'Aye, I guess that old woman wasn't so slow... '

Susan called Pepe to heel, whispered a quick, 'Take care', and strode quickly off along the overgrown path.

He raised his hand in silent farewell, but she never looked back. He stood for a time, imagining her progress through the woods. Suddenly conscious of his loneliness, he gave an involuntary shiver and began to pack up his fishing gear. Taking one last look at the river he shouldered his pack and began his journey home. Another year would soon slip by.

(In 1992, the Ballinderry River Enhancement Association was presented with a highly commended award by organisers, the Angling Foundation and the Institute of Fisheries Management, for its educational programme including field trips for local schools to the Orritor trout hatchery.)

One Enchanted Evening

by

David Graham

Phillip Caldwell was a big man, in stature, in heart, idea's everything about him was larger than life. He dressed well which tended to smooth his rugged appearance. Apart from his size, his air of quiet confidence made people look up to him. He worked for a large clothing manufacturing company and his rise to his present position as Sales Manager said something about his capabilities.

Phillip was feeling tired and irritable. The board meeting had lasted a long time and he had been shot down with every idea he'd put forward. Sales had been flagging for the past two months and the sales staff had been under pressure to do something about it. As Sales Manager he was expected to be ahead of any difficulties the staff might encounter. He had spent a lot of time mostly at home working on new methods to attract buyers in general. Not just areas that were showing a drop. He thought his solution to the problem was a good one. He had suggested that the firm employ more female sales personnel. Women, he said, had a more persuasive personality. Especially when it was mostly ladieswear they manufactured. One of the directors pointed out that there might be a discrimination factor, if they adopted that policy.

After listening to the objections and alternative suggestions he said he would give the matter more thought. After the meeting ended he left the building and got into his car parked in the staff compound and drove off thinking what do you do to convince the board that you have to try some of the things he had suggested to find out if they did work. The rejection of his ideas left Phillip feeling quite annoyed. He drove to a pub not far from the factory where he called from time to time on his way home. He parked the car and went into the bar. He usually went into the lounge but there was hardly ever anyone in there this early in the evening. He sat on a bar stool and waited while the barman finished serving another customer.

The barman came over and said, 'Good evening Mr Caldwell, the usual?'

'Yes Jim, and could you get me a sandwich.'

'Sure thing,' said the barman. 'We have cheese and tomato, egg and onion, or salad.'

'Bring me two cheese and tomato.'

82

'Right.' Said the barman, as he set him up a vodka and coke.

Phillip drank the vodka and coke while he waited for the barman to bring his sandwiches. When they arrived Phillip ordered another drink. Eating the sandwiches and sipping his drink he reflected on the days events. Things hadn't gone very well. He didn't have any backing at all at the meeting. And things weren't going too well at home recently. Alice, his wife, expected him to take more interest in things at home. He didn't see the point. They had a joint account in the bank and he had a very generous salary, which allowed her to have more or less what ever she wanted most of the time. Their two children were grown and away from home. Carson was away at law school. And Audrey was at medical school. He considered himself too busy and too involved with the firm to be bothered with trivial things, like, grass getting long round the edge of the lawn. Conservatory needing painting. Moss growing on the drive. If these things need doing get someone in to do them.

But really the problem was, Alice would have liked Phillip to pay her a bit more attention. She was getting bored with the responsibility of making all the decisions in running the home. Nothing but female company at the different committees. Even though she was in her forties she was still a very attractive woman, and needed that little bit of attention. They had been taking each other for granted and Alice was too proud to give any indication of her needs. And he too set in his ways to notice.

Phillip was sipping his fifth vodka and coke when Brian Burgess came into the bar. He saw Phillip and came over. Brian was one of the area representatives. They were on very good terms. Brian had been with the firm a long time. Almost as long as Phillip.

'What would you like to drink?' said Phillip.

'Oh, just a lager for me, have you been in here long?'

'Not all that long, the monthly board meeting didn't go all that well and it was stopping time when it was over. I came over here to get a drink and a sandwich and get the bad taste out of my mouth, anyway this is one of Alice's committee nights so there would have been no one in the house.'

The drinks arrived and the conversation went back to shop. How they could improve sales, and a general analysis of factory policy. Brian bought a round of drinks and they talked for another fifteen minutes then Brian said he had to go.

'I wouldn't drink any more Phillip I know you can take it but there's a big purge on at the moment. The law are checking drivers at random, and it wouldn't be nice to lose the car licence now would it.'

'I'm having one more and then I'm off. See you tomorrow.'

'Right, cheers,' said Brian.

Phillip finished his drink and left the pub. He walked out to his car feeling a damned sight better than when he came in. A little light headed perhaps but nothing that would do him any harm. He started the car and drove out on to the ring road which would take him round the town. He lived on the outskirts at the other side of town. The traffic had thinned out considerably. He looked at his watch. It was eight thirty. He didn't realize he had been in the pub so long. He thought, never mind, Alice won't be home from her committee meeting 'till around ten so she won't be nagging about him stopping in the pub instead of coming straight home. He came to the slip road which took him off the ring road up on to the roundabout and then to the road which took him to his street. He indicated and turned the car into the slip road. Somehow it didn't seem the same. It was much too smooth too steep, and the wrong colour. He looked in the mirror, no one behind him, he applied the brakes but the car didn't slow down it just kept going as if there were no brakes. It swept up into a large brightly lit opening and on into the centre of a vast dome like a hanger. Only there were no other vehicles in there.

Phillip got out of the car to find out what had happened. If he'd taken a wrong turning and driven into a works building. Then he remembered what happened when he had tried to apply the brakes coming up the slip road. He was wondering what to do when two sphere's with strange featured heads encased in what looked like transparent plastic converged on him from nowhere. They didn't travel very fast but they had no contact with the ground or visible means of support. When they stopped they just seemed to hover. They just stayed motionless and stared at him. Suddenly he got a clear impression of his own name, Phillip, in his mind. It happened again a few seconds later. Then words began to form as if he couldn't control his thoughts.

'Phillip. That is the designation you are known by. We are communicating by thought transference so do not be alarmed. We are the guardians of all visible universes through time up to our own time. Beyond that it is the responsibility of one's in our future.'

Phillip thought, I must be dreaming. There is no such thing as time travel.

'Oh yes there is', came the answer. 'Time is only movement. If you cease all movement within your body then you will be transported into the future unaltered until you resume movement again but travel into the future can only be done at the speed time itself travels. It's only the past that can be altered. To travel into the past is done by rotation. If you are at a given point and go to another point in no time. You will be at the two points simultaneously. If you travel faster than that, you will go back in time. We have chosen you Phillip to take our instructions to your leaders to stop you from heading this world into self destruction, and upsetting the balance of this universe which in turn would unbalance creation. We have made a list of recommendations to safeguard any of these things happening. Firstly to make sure all different fractions of your race agree. We advise that one representative from every fraction be chosen to form a collective governing body. Then make a law to banish nuclear arms. Control the production of your race to a level sufficient to ensure continuity. Stop the production of gases which will eventually destroy the natural filtration system of the sun's rays. We will not contact you again if these requests are met. If not we will have to take alternative steps.'

'What do you mean you will take alternative steps,' thought Phillip.

'We mean that if your race does not agree to take any of these precautions, it would be better the destruction of your species, than the destruction of creation. Come. We will take you back to when this world was in its glory. Before you started to misuse everything.'

The beings floated to either side of him. He felt himself floating along with them. They seemed to pass through some kind of barrier in the middle of the dome. There was no visible barrier, yet they were inside another compartment. He was guided to sit in a unit shaped like an egg shell. It closed round him when he sat down. The two beings floated to the centre of the compartment and settled into receptacles shaped to fit their carriages. There was an uneasy silence. Phillip felt very dizzy and he blacked out.

He came round to a tapping noise on the plastic dome that covered him. He found a lever at the side and turned it. The plastic slid down. The beings were gone. It was the face of a human dressed in blue looking in at him.

He said, 'Where did the beings go?'

The human in blue said, 'What did they look like?'

'They are shaped like a sphere with a head encased in plastic,' said Phillip.

'They usually take the form of an elephant, and are coloured pink,' said the constable. 'Would you mind blowing in the bag sir.'

85

Pig Trouble

by

Brian Clarke

Some thirty years ago, I spent a winter in digs in a small hamlet on the Yorkshire moors. Being bored, as there was no telly and the nearest library was a five mile hike away, on my days off, I used to help my landlord Dave on his smallholding.

I particularly liked feeding his sow, for on the day of my arrival, she had given birth to a horde of small squeaking piglets. It was impossible to count them for they ceaselessly strove for a better teat, burrowing over and under each other while mother lay there with an expression on her face which put me in mind of those notices you see outside fundamentalist gospel halls. The ones telling you; 'The Wages of Sin are Death'.

From mum's expression I gathered pay day had arrived.

On coming down to breakfast my first Saturday there, Dave, a thickset dark haired man, his handsome Gipsy looks at odds with his wife Mary's fair Viking tresses, asked me, 'I knows thee's goin' to the fair ahind pub this afternoon, but is thee doing owt this mornin' Brian?'

'Nothing in particular Dave. Why?'

'I has to ring young pigs today.'

I was intrigued, I had often seen pigs sporting nose rings, but I had never seen how they got them, so I enquired. 'How do you do it?'

Taking a large pair of pliers from the box beside his chair he placed an open wire ring in their jaws and handed them to me.

'You puts they ring in pliers like so. See how ends o they is all sharp and pointed?'

I nodded.

Placing his fingers in his nostrils he told me, 'You puts they points jist here and squeezes handles hard like.'

'Dear God that must hurt like hell,' I breathed.

'Nay. If'n you keeps fingers out o way it don't hurt a bit.' He roared with laughter at that, obviously one he'd been saving up for years.

As Dave put his coat and boots on I examined the rings. Made of shiny steel wire about the thickness of a knitting needle they were quite heavy, and when closed would be about three inches in diameter. I thought, if he puts these through the noses of those piglets the poor little sods won't be able to lift their heads off the ground.

'Aren't these too big Dave?' I asked.

Giving me my coat and an odd look he said, 'No. They's standard size.'

At the barn, he kept lambing ewes in there as well as farrowing sows, I made for the sow's pen. Heaped in a grunting pink pile, the lads were having an after breakfast snooze, blissfully unaware of the fate hanging over them.

Taking a ring from the box I held it against a tiny twitching nose. The ring was bigger than its head. Odd, still he must know what he's doing.

'Rite Brian, sheeps is all okay,' said Dave coming down the barn towards me coiling a rope round his shoulder, 'we can get on and do they pigs.'

'Okay Dave may as well start with this one,' says I.

Taking a firmer grip on the small wriggling body I held its head out to him.

He stared incredulously at me for a long moment before bursting into peals of laughter.

'Did tha' think it were they we was to do,' he gasped. 'Eh lad wait till I tells our Mary.'

Slumping against the pig pen he howled with laughter. Even Mrs Pig wore a knowing smirk. It was five minutes before he was able to stop laughing, by this time even the damned sheep had stuck their silly heads through the rails, the better to sneer at me.

When he finally recovered, Dave led me outside, over a stile, and across two fields to a third which had a small hut in one corner. The field looked as if tanks had been dirt tracking in it. I said as much.

'That's why thee puts rings in pigs noses,' he explained as we climbed over the stile. 'Stops they mucking up field.'

At the hut he opened the top half of the double door. Seven pigs, each about three feet long raised inquisitive snouts and grunted sociably, their bright beady eyes assessing us for tasty titbits. Dave explained the procedure.

He would get inside and pass one end of the rope out the window to me and then put the noose end round a pigs neck. All I had to do was hold the beast steady while he ringed it.

Looking in I saw the gang had gathered around him, doubtless hoping for an early lunch. With a dexterous flick he dropped the noose over the nearest ones head. The potential luncher objected to this by shaking its head and grunting irritably. Having tied the end of the rope around my waist I easily dealt with this by pulling the slack tight, complacently thinking to myself, this pig ringing's a doddle.

However, when Dave stuck the ring through its nose the whole scene changed dramatically, for the wretched thing went mad. Shrieking like a banshee it ran up one wall across the ceiling and down the other wall before galloping round the inside of the hut at one hundred and fifty miles per hour. Its companions, entering into the spirit of the thing, pursued it, screaming encouragement, not that it needed any.

For a brief moment, Dave stood like a lighthouse, poised amidst a surging sea of pork, before the encircling rope whisked his feet from under him. The mob, by now on their second lap, hurdled him without even breaking stride. I witnessed this from my vantage point halfway through the window where I had been dragged.

Indeed, if the rope hadn't entwined itself round Dave it would have been me on the deck as a contestant in the track and field events.

It took us five minutes to extricate ourselves and another good half hours back breaking effort before the gang were ringed.

'I didn't know pigs were so bloody athletic,' I moaned, ruefully surveying my bleeding hands.

A bedraggled Dave dolefully agreed. 'Aye. But thee weren't wrestling wi they on floor.' He looked at me, 'Ah could murder a pint. What about thee?'

I seconded the motion. Callously leaving our porcine wrestling companions to compare their new jewellery, we tottered off. As we sat quaffing a second pint comparing our wounds, the landlords wife popped her head into the snug.

'Aren't you two going to have a go at bowling for the pig?'

'We're Jewish, we're not allowed to have anything to do with pigs,' I told her firmly.

A Visit From the Devil

by

John McAuley

Four men were sitting around a table in an old shed playing cards - as had been their custom every Sunday night for over a year - in a lonely spot deep in the country. As they played, they drank whisky and smoked cigarettes continuously. Their dialogue was filthy and they told risque stories and jokes; they swore when the cards went against them - in a manner that was blasphemous.

As the night wore into early morning, two of them had dropped out. About two am on Monday, only two were still at it: One of these was Dion the habitual winner, and the worst blasphemer and filthy talker amongst them. Eventually, Dion wins again, of course, and stays behind to count his winnings and finish the whisky.

About three am, he heard a loud knock on the door; he cursed and rose to see who it was. Because he was half-drunk, he was slow and the stranger gave a shout; this brought more curses from Dion who was getting very violent by this time. After a time, he finally got the door unbolted, and the stranger pushed past him into the shed. He was a tall man with a sallow complexion, dressed in black and wearing a top-hat, which exaggerated his height.

Because Dion was drunk and in a bad mood, he shouted at the stranger and told him to 'Get to hell out of here.'

The man in black just laughed and pulled a bundle of twenty pound notes from his pocket, and said, 'I believe you have a card school going here.'

Dion, whose eyes had popped wide open at the sight of all the money, stammered, 'Ye-ye-ye-yes.'

So immediately they settled down for a game, and Dion took another swig from the bottle - just to give him courage.

Slowly the morning passed on, and Dion was losing the money he had earlier won, and he was swearing more than usual. The man in black just sat and smiled; this made Dion even more angry, and he showed antipathy for the stranger by saying: 'For Christ's sake say something and stop smiling you black bastard; I'll make you smile with the other side of your white face when my luck changes.'

Then Dion proceeded to boast to the stranger about all the money he had won from his friends in the past, and tried to make him lose concentration - but to no avail. This invidious behaviour only made the stranger finish each game faster.

Soon all Dion's money was lost; he put his face in his cupped hands and cried and cursed. Still the stranger just sat quietly and smiled sardonically.

Eventually, the man in black spoke for the first time since he had started to play.

'I'll give you one more chance to win your money back - with interest.'

'But I don't have any money left to play with.'

'That's all right, I'll play you for your soul against all the money I have - one game.'

Dion couldn't believe his ears; he thought that the man was mad, and laughed until the tears ran down his face.

'Right,' Dion said, 'my soul against all your money. I have nothing to lose, anyway.' And laughed again, 'you must be mad or an imbecile.'

So the stranger started to deal the cards, but Dion would not agree to this because he thought the stranger was a cheat, and he told him so, and he insisted on dealing the cards himself.

It was a long game but at last it was over with the same result as before. This time Dion laughed himself silly, and told the stranger that he could not take his soul, and he made fun of him for playing for such a foolish stake.

'You have an impuissant mind to think you can take my soul.'

Just then a gust of wind blew through a broken window, and blew the joker on to the floor, below the table. Dion, still laughing, got down on his knees to pick up the card, and to his horror saw two cloven hooves where the stranger's feet should have been.

He gasped, panted for breath, clutched his chest, and made a loud painful guttural sound, fell over on his side, gave a twitch or two - and was dead.

The stranger rose; lifted his hat; scratched his horns; because he was not accustomed to wearing it, his horns had become itchy. He placed the man's money on the corpse and walked out - still smiling to himself.

On the following Monday morning, at around about eleven o'clock, Dion's wife went around to Ben's house to see if he knew where Dion was. Ben was surprised that he had not been home, and said that he would go and look for him. He went and got his two gambling associates, Elliott and Barry, and they all went out to the old shed, deep in the country, to look for Dion.

They found him lying on the floor.

'Get up you drunken old fool; it's almost noon on Monday, and your wife's looking for you.'

When they got no response, Barry kicked Dion gently on the stomach, and from the touch he knew Dion was dead.

'I think he's dead.'

They turned him over and found it so. Since they were such an indurated lot of slime, they searched Dion's pockets and shared all his money amongst themselves. They never, for a second, thought about the hardship his wife should have to bear with the funeral expenses and two young kids to bring up. All they could think about was the game on the following Sunday night.

On the following Wednesday, at the funeral, all they did was plan and talk about the big game, the meeting time, and the sort of drink to buy.

On the Sunday night, each started the game with great expectations; each thought he was going to win all the money.

After several hours of vile argumentative gambling, two o'clock Monday morning saw Ben the winner; the other two left him on his own to count his takings and finish the drink.

When, to his surprise, there was a loud bang on the door and a shout to open-up. For a minute, Ben thought who it may be: was it robbers, or was it the police, or was it his wife come to fetch him home.

After the usual swearing, he managed to get the door opened, and to his great surprise, he saw a tall dark stranger dressed in black and wearing a top hat.

'What the f--- hell do you want; f--- off you black bastard,' cursed Ben.

But the stranger stood his ground and smiled.

'I believe you have a card school going here.' Producing a wad of notes from his pocket.

Ben's face lit up with avaricious delight when he saw the money.

'Come in Sir!' He cried, and shook the stranger's hand. 'I'm the only one left, but I have all the money and I'll play you.

The stranger entered the shed smiling sardonically to himself, and seated himself at the old table.

And the game began in earnest.

The Shadow of the Mills

by

Gerry Oates

'Here's an ad' for a bike,' announced my Da as he poured over the paper at the tea table. 'A Hercules, an' it's only a couple of years old.'

'Where?' My Ma demanded.

'Here in 'The Telegraph'.'

'No. I mean where are they sellin' it from?'

'Westmoreland Street.'

'But that's off the Shankill Road', interrupted my uncle Joe who was stayin' with us at the time.

'Well', snapped my Da, 'they won't ate us, will they?'

When the dishes had been cleared and my Ma was busy tidying up in the scullery, my Da got up from the table and put on his cap.

'I think I'll take a walk over there an' have a look at that bike. Are you comin'?' he said, indicating me. I wasn't sure if I wanted to go or not, but curiosity overcame fear and I said 'Yes.'

I had never been in a Protestant house before. Of course, I had seen them before, on The Twelfth, when my Da took me to see the bands and, downtown, at least half the people you passed in the street must've been 'Prods'. But I had never spoken to one. What would they be like, I wondered, as I got ready; would they know I was a 'Mickey'? What would I do if they asked me what I was? Would I deny my faith? Had I the mettle of the martyrs who had died for the Faith? As a child, I had dreaded such a situation where I would have to choose between life and denying the Faith. My mind shuffled these questions through my childish head as I laced my boots with an unsteady hand and prepared to face the unknown.

We left Albert Street behind and crossed The Falls into Northumberland Street, a dark, forbidding street in the shadow of the mills, Craig's on one side and Isaac Andrews' on the other. There were no houses in the street until you got to the bend where the mill buildings ended and then you had the familiar red-brick, terrace houses just like Albert Street behind us. When we had passed the mills we were in Protestant territory; it was like that all along The Falls - Andrews', Craig's, Greaves's, Coombe-Barbour's and Ross's Mill all marked the end of one territory and the beginning of another; at the other end of Albert Street, too, The Durham Flax Spinning Mill drew a line between Catholic and Protestant.

'That's not a Catholic church, sure it isn't, Da?' I asked as we passed St Luke's on our right.

'No, Jimmy, it's not. It belongs to The Church of Ireland.'

'But St Luke was a Catholic, wasn't he?'

'He was,' replied my Da, a little uncertain of his ground.

'Then why have the Protestants called a church after him?'

'Eh, there were no Protestants then, only eh... '

'Only Catholics?' I suggested.

'Yes, but they didn't call them Catholics then.'

'What did they call them?'

'Christians, Jimmy, they called them Christians... Watch out! There's a bus comin'. It's a '77', that's The Waterworks - Gasworks route. That's another route number you can add to your collection. How many have you now?'

'That makes eighteen, I think,' I answered and all thoughts about St Luke and his religious persuasion vanished as quickly as they had appeared.

We crossed Northumberland Street when the bus had gone, passed Cumberland Street and turned into a long, narrow street, just like our own, with lots of little streets crossing it at intervals; this was Westmoreland Street. It ran parallel to the Shankill and the mere sound of that name struck terror in me. I didn't know the Shankill, I'd heard about The Hammer and The Nick, but I had no idea where these districts were and wondered what they called this area. Many years later when I was trying my luck with a girl from Penrith Street I used to think they should've called this area The Lake District, like they did with The Holy Land on the other side of town, for there was a Kendal Street and a Lorton Street as well.

'We've come about the bike,' said my Da when a cheerful-looking woman answered the door.

She invited us in and shouted upstairs: 'Ernie, there's someone come about the bike.'

It was a simple kitchen house with a cosy fire burning in the Devon grate, the wireless was on. There were two young lads, both older than me, playing with a big, black Labrador on the sofa and when the man came downstairs they went suddenly quiet and the dog was put in the yard.

'Hold on a minute, mister,' said the man, 'an' I'll wheel it in till ye see it; it's in the 'shade' out the back.' The woman spread a newspaper on the floor and the

93

bike was turned upside down with its handlebars and saddle on the sheet of paper. My Da turned the pedals by hand and checked the chain. The bike was then set back its proper way.

'Do you want to take a spin on her to see what she's like?' The man asked.

'I'll just take her to the top of the street,' said my Da.

I was suddenly alone and ill at ease in a strange house, a Protestant house, too. It was much like ours, only there was no Sacred Heart picture on the wall; instead, a framed photograph of The King and Queen hung over the fireplace. On the wall behind the sofa there was a strange picture with a ladder on it and a six-pointed star and several other symbols I couldn't make out.

'Are you at school, son?' the woman asked.

'I am.'

'What book are you in?'

'Pardon?'

'What class are you in?'

'Third. But I'll be movin' into Fourth after the holidays.'

'I suppose you like school, do you?'

'Sometimes,' I answered, not wishing to get involved in a long debate, and was glad to see my Da come back to take over the burden of conversation. He talked to the man at the door for a minute and they shook hands.

'Yous'll take a sup of 'tay' before yous leave,' said the woman.

'Of course they will,' the man answered for us and the woman brought us tea and fresh soda farls from the scullery.

'Is this your big fella, then?' said the man taking notice of me for the first time. He put his hand in his pocket and reached me a shilling. 'Here, put that in yer money box when you get home.' My eyes turned the size of soup plates at the sight of the shining, silver coin as I felt it in my hand. I'd never owned a shilling before and I couldn't keep my hands off it, checking it was still in my trouser pocket every half-minute and fumbling with it between my fingers.

It was eight o'clock when we left that house in Westmoreland Street. It was a bright, summer night and my Da put me on the bar and cycled home through the side streets. When we reached the main road he got off and made me walk while he wheeled the bike.

'Why did we get off, Da?' I asked.

'The cops would take your name if they caught you on the bar.'

'Why's that?'

'It's not allowed. You're not supposed to give anyone a ride on the bar,' he explained.

94

We left the mills behind and crossed into our own territory once again. From Westmoreland Street to Milford Street was less than half-a-mile, but there was more than distance and the menacing shadow of the mills that separated the two.

'I got the bike for thirty bob,' my Da announced proudly as he pushed open the kitchen door and wheeled it in.

'Do you think you got a bargain?' my Ma asked him.

'No doubt about it. Just look at 'er, she's like the day she came out of the shop, an' there's a pump with 'er as well.'

'An' the man give me a shillin',' I shouted showing off my brand new coin.

'Did he knew what yous were?' enquired Uncle Joe who was hovering over the fire with 'The Telegraph' between his hands.

'Of course he did,' replied my Da sharply. 'Everybody in Northern Ireland knows what everybody else is. It only takes twenty seconds of conversation to find that out.'

Black and White

by

Maureen Campbell

The dress hangs ghostly, like an abstract pattern in the darks and blacks of the surrounding cubes. Blocks of light and shade. Her Art teacher had called it chiaroscuro. Sarah scrunches bare toes in the fleece of an ethereal, vividly remembered, bedside rug. Her legs are pale like the dress but not so startling against the shadowy cream of the rug and the tossed sheets. She can't sleep. Excitement. Anxiety. The anticipation of her beginning rumbles and rattles and careers like a playful kitten. Black and white. Black panes edged pale. Moonlight splitting jet leaving shadows in between. The grey areas? Were there doubts?

The difference between right and wrong. Right to do as she was doing. Wrong to leave her aged parents? Plump, pink motherly mother. Bustling and busy, always active. Charged with the day to day currents of polish and pots and practicalities. Gentle, slow-moving father with his shy smile and scholarly artistry. Smoothing eyebrows that bristled over far-seeing blue as he dreamed his dreams and smiled into the distance of his thoughts. Opposites. Black and white. But one in their blanketing love and simple hopes for their only daughter. Smothering. Binding. Sarah longs for white freedom. The price, lonely darkness and the draining of colour from them. She had thought at one time that they would welcome her decision. The blessing of the blessed virgin on their child. But they were old. No longer able to depend on each other, their mutual comforting staled and bleached. They swam in chains. The only certainty, death. The final blackness.

Tomorrow Sarah would bring that blackness closer. Tomorrow they would fix white smiles to pale lips and the dark shadows of their eyes would search the other's for understanding. The white flowers that spoke of love and spring and rebirth would only shout emptiness, their deathly pallor. Indeed there were doubts. But not her own. Sarah was sure. The indisputable dogmatism of youth. And love. Love given, love received, love forever enfolding. Love, that was the white path to freedom, yet black was her goal.

Ivory fingers of moonlight flit across bed and dresser and hanging folds of pearl. Sarah kneels before the black transparency of the window. Alabaster reflections stare softly from the depths. 'For we see through a glass darkly.' But tomorrow I will know, she breaths and her face fades in the mist of breath.

Fair dark head on pale arms Sarah vaguely views through closed eyes the particles of her childhood. White sand trickling through white toes. The long anticipated holiday had begun. Soon the white heat of the yellow sun would change her skin from sickly pink to healthy glowing. White curls of froth sent shivers as feet half sunk in wet sand waited for the fierce thrill of gushing sea. Her friend Patsy had gone with them one summer. For days that seemed like centuries the two had envisaged. Sitting like crows on the railings of the park, chittering.

Stretched on the smelly, leather seats of empty, green and yellow buses in the closed depot, for privacy.

'Tell me again about the beach, Sarah.' And Sarah, superior in her knowledge of the childhood seaside obliged. 'How high do the waves go, Sarah? Can you really walk about in your bare feet?' The clear, translucent remembrances were transmitted over and over again.

But, where Sarah savoured softness, Patsy found only grainy discomfort. Hair-tugging wind elated, with the other it distressed. A sudden, strange, male scent beckoned in the new-found freedom. But Sarah's seduction came from another direction. Until disagreement whittled and wore at the friendship. Within a week the familiarity was lost in alien territory. The similarity of years eroded by the differences. No longer friends now, twelve years on. Nor enemies. Just opposites. Black and white.

Then the dark, dreary days of Lent. The Fast. The dark, early morning Mass and the brightness of the kitchen. White table-cloth illumined in the fire-light. Pulled closer for comfort. And the dark avenue to school. Evening dark too, rehearsing for Reverend Mother's feast day. 'Sarah has a lovely voice.' It echoed in vestal purity though the gloom of chapel. It had to lighten their way along hidden roads. High yellow lamps flickering greenly through whispering foliage. Frightening. They sang to warble away the fear, clasping Burberries with gloved, sticky hands. Staying close. Into the dazzling of the town. The blue-black sky recedes behind cold, yet friendly now, the white glares of street lights.

Sarah dreams she is in another place. A gentle tap, tentative, uncertain sends Sarah scurrying silently to the tangle of kicked off sheets. Her mother's whisper seeks entry, pleading, desperate. Sarah welcomes cheerily, white face illumined, bright in the artificial brightness of the switched-on lamp.

'I wanted...' Sarah's brightness flickers in the face of wrinkled confusion. 'I wanted to make sure...'

'I'm fine, mother, I'm happy and I'm sure.' But words can bring no comfort. Childless loneliness stretches. The heart is worn with the caring and the loving and the soon to be missing. And no sharing. Flesh of her flesh, yet might just as well be incarcerated behind impenetrable ice. Sarah's hands, milky tinged peach in the light's glow hold fast to her mother's spotted, shiny ones. But, neither can touch, nor sight nor hearing cure the aching sickness. Nor press life's blood back into the wilting flower of motherhood. The old woman's eyes pray. Don't go, wafts on the air like a recalcitrant dust-mite. Sarah smiles her sorrow, yet redefines her happiness.

Another withered hand insinuates itself around the mother's stooped shoulders. Blue eyes unhappy in their present, wishing for the past, shine wetly in to Sarah's. 'Goodnight love, and God bless.' He gently steers. Understanding, agreeing, but guilty in their sadness.

A sudden wall of sable falls. She is awake. Enfolded in the warm darkness. Welcoming, unafraid, she wallows in the charcoal smudge. Sarah breathes the night. Black is where she wants to be. The soft, soothing depth of no light. Presently the shapes return. Marble streaks of moonshine lifts the shadows without displaying the unwanted corners. Sarah remembers again. The flashing on and off at juvenile parties. 'Switch off the light!' hissed from struggling depths of sweaty corners. The sudden, electrifying flash that illuminated shame and fright with the arrival of a parent. The blind eye turned when Peter was partner. Her mother had a closeness with his mother. A shared ambition. There had been the half-grasped hope that he would be the one. Had she ever pleased them? Even now, she wonders. A minute tarnish mars her future. The silver sheen blackened. But Peter was not her future. She was art, he was science. Her parents would have known in time. Opposites. Attraction without depth. Black and white.

Pleasing pushes memory through. Sarah had pleased once. Her ambition once had coincided with theirs. Mingled, emerged prideful. Their daughter the teacher. For once in line with their hopes. Their shining joy fulfilled in graduation. Then, shortly, her choices puzzled, dismayed. Yet the abstraction was, should have been a bright, shimmering joy. They hid in darkness from her future. Unable to accept the separation. The black chasm of their apartness. Alien, unknown. The dirty urchins learning of Van Gogh. Tanned by the artists suns and disbelieving of the lore. They had been Sarah's future. They still would be. Though the dirt would be inkier, more ebony, eventually.

Sarah sighs. Her heart battles for the joy she knows will come. Is it a selfish joy? Should filial debts and duties mask the bright stones of her path? A leaden greyness steals across her knowing. Her moon-bleached hair falls heavily but is quickly pushed aside with the doubts. There are no choices. No grey area. Only black and white. And Sarah has chosen. Tomorrow. Only death, her own, can change what lies ahead.

'It still isn't too late to change your mind.' Her mother's whispering voice echoes achingly through the peaceful dark. Reprieve? But the sunny days of childhood have sunk below the horizon of twilight. Obscured in the dim caverns of adulthood. Womanhood. That voice that once soothed and gentled and scolded and taught is weakened by the clouds of time. Blotted out by the brilliance of her own certainty. Another voice is stronger. Eclipsing all else. Her mother's voice cries, stay. The other, come. Tomorrow Sarah will go. Her mind or heart will not change. The only change will be her name.

As milky strands of dawn stretch grasping fingers to the day Sarah stirs. Cream ripples of hair are pushed aside, along with the lack-lustre spectre of her night-time thoughts. The white dress hangs bridal now. A weak sun licks its floury folds. A foretaste of the radiant white-heat to come. Today! Pale cheeks bloom as virgin fabric enfolds. Today! Sarah pulls impatiently at the abundant glory of her silken hair. The symbol of her past. She wishes speed to the silver flash that will propel her to her future. Soon. The white will change to black. The colour of her future. Bridal black. Soon she will don the mantle of her wedded life. Today she will leave Sarah behind. Forever to be known as Sister Benedict.

Black Widows and Flourishing Corn

by

Linda Erwin

A picture of my grandparents hangs on my bedroom wall and to this day, as I look at it, it instils in me a sense of calm in my periods of rest. Her smiling face like Queen Victoria's, though softened and shaded with inner light: his, a strong humorous face with deep laughter lines and eyes that suggest a twinkle. And yet my childhood memories are a mixture of affection for them, and terror of the circumstances I found myself in after he had died and she, pining and alone, had made 'the arrangement' with my parents. It was that my big sister and I should take it night about to sleep over at granny's wee white washed cottage at the bottom of our yard.

Unfortunately the thick blackstone walls, low ceilings and stone floors of the cottage seemed to act as a magnet for spiders, cockroaches and beetles the size of small mice. Nearly every night when I went to bed, there was a great black spider clinging tentatively to the bedroom ceiling, ready to drop onto my face as soon as I got between the sheets. My initial scream usually brought Granny tutting and teetering unsteadily with the aid of her stick up to the room, already armed with a rolled up copy of the People's Friend. With a deft flick of the magazine she landed the unfortunate beastie into the chamber pot under the bed to suffer a watery demise. Once the lights were out and I was in bed there was no guarantee that another creepy crawlie might not climb up the sheets and attack. In the end my only escape was to bury myself under the blankets until I was too tired to resist, and sleep released me from my terror.

Granny was the typical product of the late 1800's in Northern Ireland - all white lace and black-buckled shoes in the old sepia photographs of her youth, perfect posture, expression poised and prim. At the age of eighty she had long, straight, silver-grey hair rolled up in a neat little bun at the back, and wore black and grey garments that covered her from head to toe. She had a strange rounded shape which I discovered to be the result of a large flannel wrap that circled her midriff several times, removing all semblance of shape summer and winter alike. Its purpose escaped me and somehow it seemed impolite to ask. She was a very religious woman, and one of my nightly tasks was to read to her

100

from the bible as she rocked to and fro on the old wooden rocker by the Aga stove, door ajar and coal glowing crimson on cold winter nights.

Before granda's death the house had been a meeting place for all the farmers who lived nearby. It contained a little shop at one end with a very strange assortment of goods; large sacks of flour and potatoes, shelves full of tins with rusty rims, and a huge piece of salted ling fish that hung from a nail on the back of the shop door. It was more like a store than a shop and was yet another breeding ground for the insipient insect population. The shop's customers all seemed to be over seventy and came more for 'the crack' than the goods. The men all had double-barrelled names like William-James and Robert-Hugh and they all came on foot, sometimes from several miles hence. My granda was full of stories and granny would pretend not to approve of his wicked sense of humour.

The lane opposite granny's house was lined with bushes of flourishing corn that came into bloom every summer. The scent of it always reminds me of those heady days of youth when I used to pick bunches of wild flowers to set on her sideboard. I would ride my bicycle round the yard making up religious poems which I would read to her later. They usually contained references to Zion and the pearly gates and I doubt if they made sense, but she always approved and encouraged me in my efforts.

The arrangement lasted several years throughout the mid-sixties and took me through to the pains and traumas of emerging pubescence. My arachnaphobia stayed with me but was now accompanied by a nocturnal yearning to grow breasts. I had read somewhere that rubbing cold tea-leaves on the chest could achieve startling results, and so I frequently sneaked some from the teapot at home and put the theory to the test. It was a messy business, but they did eventually appear!

I will never forget my last night of sleeping over at granny's. She hadn't been well all that day, but when I offered to fetch my mother she just sighed and said that she didn't want to be a bother. I lay awake for hours listening to her rasping breath and rattling chest and I prayed that she wouldn't die on me there and then. Eventually, at around three a.m. she asked me weakly to go and get my parents.

The yard between my own house and granny's held numerous terrors in the dark. We lived on a pig farm and the piggeries were just down the lane. Rats were sometimes a problem and each night in pitch darkness the mad dash from my back door to granny's front door was of an Olympic standard! Open meal stores, shed doorways and the peat-house were Hamlynesque black holes. That night I had to bang on the back door, then the front door, and eventually throw stones at my parents' window before I made it to the safety of my own beloved bed.

Granny died two days later and I never saw her again. I missed her dearly and to this day my memories are of warm glowing nights and a godly peace and serenity. The creepie crawlies seem smaller and less threatening now, but the scent of the flourishing corn is still as strong and as sweet as ever it was.

A Coincidental Accident

by

Keith Miller

My dad has often spoken of an incident he witnessed, as a teenager, in the early sixties. In those days motor-cars were few and far between on the roads of Banbridge town, an even more obscure sight around the scattering of villages on its out-skirts. This of course was the primary reason for the accident being regarded as such an event; but there was more to it than that. Something had occurred which was so coincidental as to assure it a place in our provinces history.

Every Saturday evening he and his three mates would set off from the village of Seapatrick along the one mile path leading to Peal's pub in Banbridge. They would drink for several hours at this establishment, which also functioned as a funeral parlour and failing brewery, before staggering back to their various homes.

The ambience in the bar, on the night of my dad's tale, was slightly more jovial than usual. This was due to Neil Peal giving out free beer. Perhaps I should explain that, although Neil had many fine aspects to his personality, being exceptionally giving wasn't one of them. Tonight, he was attempting to wean his customers off the more expensive imported brand, more expensive for him that is, and acquaint them with his own latest homemade brew. It was a last ditch effort to sell his own commodity. Unfortunately though, and apparently unbeknown to him, it tasted much the same as every other beer he had ever produced; pitiful.

Mark, a close friend of dads and tight ass of some renown, was so taken with his idea of free booze, taste to him being no object, that he gave his evening to guzzling the stuff like tap water. When Neil's antique grandfather clock struck midnight, Mark was on the verge of clobbering anyone who so much as came within swinging distance.

His mates, having discussed their predicament over one last pint of the imported brand, decided there was nothing else for it but to tell his da; Mr Paxon had, after all, the only car in Seapatrick. He would give his son a damn good thrashing once he got him home but, in Mark's belligerent state of intoxication, there was no way they could have walked him to the village.

103

Shortly after his friends left, Mark decided to follow suit. If he hurried, and caught up with them, he knew, instinctively, that he would be preventing a great deal of unpleasantness with his father.

Lady luck was on his side; or so he thought.

No sooner did he stumble from Peal's, sobered slightly by the urgency of his task, than a car had screeched to a halt alongside of him. The driver was signalling for him to get in. He did. As the young man fiddled with the ignition, Mark enquired if he knew the whereabouts of Seapatrick. His reply, albeit incoherent, was obviously a positive one.

The roar of an engine distracted the three from their conversation and drew their attention back to town. A red Mini, which couldn't have been travelling at any less than seventy miles an hour, was criss-crossing its way along the broken white line in the centre of the road. In disbelief, they watched it leap onto the footpath opposite, skid through Mary Pepper's garden, and accelerate towards them.

Before he dove, my dad can distinctly recall seeing Mark's horrified visage gazing from the passenger side; he had become a caricature of his former self, all eyes and mouth.

The little Mini bounded the kerb and hurled itself through the topiary hedge surrounding Doctor Dale's landscaped garden. One of his clipped eagles flew skyward on impact, or perhaps the bird took flight deliberately rather than witness the senseless destruction of natural beauty. Ruby red roses, breathtakingly beautiful tulips, and the most marvellous marigolds were indiscriminately slaughtered. The remaining eagle, perching proudly in its designated corner, was also catapulted to the mercies of the night, as the hedge beneath it exploded into a cloud of tiny green leaves and broken branches.

Each of the boys were struggling to their feet when the shower of hedge clippings came raining down on them. In stunned silence, they peered through the airborne foliage at the automobile hurtling along the pavement, en route to Seapatrick; a pavement which, for the next quarter of a mile, lay adjacent to an entire row of occupied houses.

Mark, more sober than at any time in his entire life, was busy telling the driver to stop the car, this was the street he lived on, when he suddenly noticed, lit up in the beams thrown from the headlights, Will Cairn's dog, Harold. The driver, miraculously seeing him also, and rather than do an emergency stop, spun violently on the steering wheel in an effort to swerve the overweight beagle. He was too slow. Harold was whisked between the wheels with an ear splitting howl. Then Mark found himself screaming in unison, as his eyes fell upon the house that was rushing towards them.

The mini, crumpling by about twenty-five per cent on impact, sent an entire mahogany door rocketing down a hallway, and smashing into a china cabinet in the living room. It was a cabinet filled with every trophy Mark's dad had ever won as an amateur footballer.

My own dad, and his two companions, arrived on the scene seconds before Mark flung himself from the wreckage, tripping over a rather irate beagle as he did so. Mr Paxon was in hot pursuit. None of the boys could quite catch what it was he was yelling, but the broken brass football cup, being manically waved above his head, told of his intentions with much more eloquence than he ever could.

It came as no great surprise for them to find that the driver had also vacated the mini. Joyriders often flee the stolen vehicle following such incidents. What did surprise them however, as it did everyone else in the village, was the fact that the car, being the only one owned in Seapatrick, should have collided with the owners house.

Guests of Gallows Hill

by

Alexander Bailie

A ghostly place is Gallows Hill,
Where a gibbet creaks and the air grows chill.
For underneath swings a gruesome figure,
Slow at first, then with vigour.
Shadows shape with nights embrace,
For the light of day they cannot face.
But darkness woos them like a lover,
Within its depth they float and hover.
Dark forces 'tis best to leave alone,
For they're not of blood, flesh nor bone.
Forever present, restless still,
Just like the guests of Gallows Hill.

The weather had changed dramatically. It started to rain heavily, and the muffled sound of thunder could be heard along the coast of Strangford Lough.

The two young men cycled side by side, each with their own thoughts. What had been a fine, sunny morning as they had journeyed, was now a bleak, grey evening, with night descending.

'We will have to find somewhere out of this,' said John.

'Yes, it looks like its on for the night,' replied Steve. They pushed on steadily through the falling rain. Just ahead of them on a hill, but some distance off the road, stood an old house. Through the gathering darkness a light glowed from a downstairs window.

'Lets see if they do bed and breakfast,' suggested John. Steve nodded. They left their bicycles propped against an aged oak tree which stood near the pathway to the house. Slowly they turned and walked in the direction of the light. Suddenly they stopped, their eyes transfixed upon a signpost, which stood about twelve feet high.... a gruesome sight From its rusty chain suspended the shape of a man carved from wood.

'Real eerie,' remarked Steve.

'Isn't it just,' agreed John.

The chain around the shape's neck creaked and swung slowly.

106

'There's something about this place I don't like,' said Steve in a disturbed manner. 'Lets move on and try somewhere else.'

'I think its alright,' replied John.

Steve felt uneasy. 'But its real weird,' he said and he shuddered.

'Look, lets not argue,' pleaded John. 'Its getting late and we'll soon be soaked to the skin.'

They felt cold and miserable, just like their surroundings. As they grew nearer to the front door of the house, they could make out the lettering on a brass plate which read Gallows Hall.

Before Steve could make any further protest, John gave the door a loud knock, but there was no answer. He waited for a minute or two before he knocked a second time. It seemed even louder to Steve. This time however they could hear movement from within. It sounded like that of heavy footsteps on a stone floor, drawing nearer to the door. Then they heard the squeaking sound of a bar being withdrawn from its bolt. The door gradually inched open and a face came into view. It was that of an old man who eyed them with suspicion in the light of a lantern, which he held aloft.

'Would it be shelter you're after?' He asked knowingly, as if he could read their minds.

'Why yes,' replied John, 'As a matter of fact we are.'

'Then lads, lets be having ye out of the rain,' said the old fellow. Having closed the door, he led them along a narrow hall into a small room, where a coal fire blazed upon its hearth, so bright that the lantern was not really needed. Steve and John stood beside the fire, their clothes quickly steaming from the heat.

The old man spoke again. 'Who might ye be, and where be ye from?' he asked curiously.

John told him briefly about themselves. But Steve did not hear him, as he was struck with awe at the old man's appearance. It was that of a pirate. From the two heavy gold rings which dangled from his ears, to the high sea boots that his trousers were tucked into. The old man had listened to John but sensed Steve's steady gaze upon him.

'Tis Silas Carveve I be, retired ships carpenter, from the brig 'Monsoon', said the old fellow, as he invited them to sit on either of the two old armchairs close to the fire. From outside there came a sudden, violent splattering of rain against the window of the room, and they could hear the faint creaking of the swinging sign. Silas looked at John and Steve, and laughed softly.

'You've been wondering about the sign of the hanging man, have ye not? he asked them.

'Yes, what's the idea of it?' quizzed Steve, for the beastly thing was getting on his nerves.

'Tis an effigy of one of me guests, named Tusker Joe, and him with not a tooth in his head', Silas replied, and whilst he chuckled told them, 'Silas, says he to me, thou could do me a great kindness, if you could carve me a likeness and hang me high, for if ever a rogue deserved hanging, it were me?

John looked at Steve and had to smile, for he was rigid, and seemed unable to speak.

'It was you made the figure, wasn't it?' asked John.

'Carveve be me name, and to carve be me nature,' answered Silas with a mischievous grin.

Outside the wind was blowing fitfully, driving rain against the window in sudden, savage bursts.

'Would it be alright if we slept here? The armchairs would be just fine', John asked.

'We would be willing to pay,' added Steve.

'Stay here if ye've mind to,' Old Silas replied. 'Yer company be pay enough.'

'Thanks ever so much,' answered John.

They both felt somewhat relieved.

Silas eyed them respectfully as he spoke. 'Tis tired ye both must be, so I think I'll let ye rest.' Lifting the lantern from the table, he gave them a long, last look. 'Sleep well', he said, and left the room, as they both wished him goodnight. They were so tired and drowsy that they fell asleep.

They both woke to the sound of early morning traffic on the Shore Road. Quickly, but quietly they left the house. Walking briskly, they lifted their bicycles from against the tree, and wheeled them down onto the footpath beside the road. They stood looking back in disbelief. The signpost that they could see was indeed old, but now nailed to it was a large For Sale notice, and from it's decayed appearance, it left no doubt in their minds it had been there for many years.

'Gallows Hill', said a voice behind them. It was that of the postman. 'For thirty years', he continued, 'I've been delivering mail around this area, and no one has lived there in all that time. Some people would try to tell you its haunted.'

Steve and John exchanged glances. 'We will', they exclaimed together. The postman listened.

Too Perfect

by

Tara McHugh

Why did I do it I ask myself now? How could I have done such an evil thing to such an innocent creature of Gods creation? Why I ask myself again and again. Why oh why?

I sit here alone, trembling at the thought of it. I still hear the blood curdling cry, and I still hear the muffled sound of her tears. As I close my eyes I see it all, the expression on her face. She lay there so peacefully, her face so white, her innocent eyes stared into nothingness. As I became conscious of myself I realized her delicate neck was still hanging limp and lifeless in my hands.

I could only cry tears of pain, tears of hurt, tears of inordinate quiet and yet deep in the recess of my troubled heart I knew I'd done the right and only humane thing I could have done.

The rattle of keys brought me out of my recurring nightmare and two policemen stood in front of me.

'You ready to talk now', one snarled at me and I just lowered my head in silence. I wanted to die. I wanted to hold my baby again, to kiss her and tell her how much I loved her. My whole body ached from the yearning.

'Why did you do it?' The policeman snarled again. I slowly lifted my head and through the tears I tried to focus on the face of the speaker.

'I did it,' I said weakly 'Because I loved her, more than anything in this world.'

They both laughed a horrible guttural laugh, half forced, half sneering, that reviled and revolted me. 'You'll go down for life you know,' he said and they left the room.

I was vaguely glad to see them go, to be alone with my thoughts. Where did all this go wrong? Where did the dream end and the nightmare begin? The midwife's voice kept repeating in my ears, 'I'm sorry, but your baby is handicapped, seriously handicapped,' and her voice trailed on and on.

I wasn't really listening to her because I was holding the most beautiful baby in the world. 'She's beautiful, just beautiful.'

'She's handicapped, brain-damaged,' the midwife repeated. 'You'll have to consider her future. There will be a counsellor who will call with you in the morning and discuss this with you.' And she left me holding my baby.

She was so tiny and fragile. I held her and cried. I cried the most stinging tears I ever cried in my life. Slowly, slowly like a grey cold mist creeping down over the mountains, realization of what the midwife had said to me began to sink in.

'Handicapped, brain-damaged', I kept repeating this to myself as I looked at my baby, I could not believe it, I just could not believe it.

In the morning the counsellor came, and the social worker and the doctor and as each came and went the midwife stood behind me saying, 'Yes handicapped, brain-damaged,' until I could stand it no longer.

They kept referring to my baby as *It* and several times I interrupted them saying, 'Her name is Orca', but again and again they would call her *It*'.

When they left I tried to think it through. Why had God chosen me to undertake this challenge! My life had been a total disaster. When I discovered I was pregnant I thought it was the worst thing that could have happened to me, no job, no man, no money. I thought about abortion but still that was too much. And then quite surprisingly, I found that I enjoyed being pregnant. I thought this baby might give me something I've never had before, someone I could love and someone who could love me. And for the first time in my life I was happy.

Now they want my baby to go into an institution. They say I am an 'Unfit mother'. But it is up to me to decide what is best for her. I know the life I would give her may not be the best but at least she would get my undivided attention. As I thought it through, I thought of death each time, I would always put it to the back of my mind, but again and again it would haunt me. I began to think that maybe this is what God wanted me to do. Maybe he also thought that this is also a challenge. He maybe thought that now it was too big for me. Maybe he had punished me enough for my sins, in the end I decided I could not go through with such an evil thing. I decided I would look after her. I emptied my mind of all the wicked things but each time death would creep back.

Later when I was discharged from hospital I decided to get her christened Orca Mary as all through the pregnancy I prayed to Mary asking her to inspire me. In a few days my little girl would be a member of the church, she would be recognised as Gods child, not as a failure or a mistake but a special child.

I had put Orca to bed and sat down to relax and to read a book. The thought of death crept back this time not frightening me. I began to think seriously about it. Maybe she was too perfect to live in this cruel, deceitful world. I

110

walked up the stairs and into the bedroom and picked her up. She had a pale complexion and her lacy nightdress draped beautifully over her tiny perfect body. My heart was beating rapidly as I kissed her head. When I told her I loved her she seemed to twitch as if to tell me she understood.

'I'm doing this out of love,' I said quietly, 'This world is not good enough for you.' I slowly laid her head on the soft white pillow and I pulled up the covers. Then I put my hands round her delicate neck. My eyes filled with tears as I gently squeezed, pressing harder and harder. Bitter stinging tears burned through my tightly closed eyes.

'Oh God let it happen quickly, quickly, let her die quickly please.' Quietly Orca began to sniffle, then her cries got louder, suddenly there was nothing. I began to release my grip but I heard a cry, it was a long continuous shriek, the like of which I had never heard before, I forced my hands around her neck to stop the cry. I felt the blood in my veins begin to curdle. I had done it, I had killed my little Orca, she maybe would be happy now. I looked at her, she lay there so peacefully, her face white and her innocent eyes stared into nothingness.

Personal Mythology

by

Bernadette McGarry

The cold grey morning gave vent to its gloomy promise and released a silent and measured fall of snow over the little grouping of shops and houses that was the town of Portstewart. Bravely facing the raw Atlantic, the town was sheltered by the towering cliffs of the north Antrim coast; Mussenden Temple on its left, dreaming of the warm Italian springs which inspired the faintly odd Earl of Bristol to position it teetering on the edge of solid basalt centuries ago, facing Benbane Head on its right, whose challenging stare of defiance had gone unheeded for much longer. The town usually escaped such wintry dramatics, preferring to inflict on its people a screaming succession of howling winds, days when the foam from the Atlantic breakers coated footpaths and buildings with sea-snow.

An angry wind, not from the sea which slept blackly this day, but inexplicably from the centre of the town itself had begun its accompaniment slowly, but had soon risen to a raging crescendo, rattling the windows of the town-hall where stiff-lipped councillors argued over the possible usage of the new community hall. Councillor Leeson who had the floor continued proposing a dinner-dance on the evening of the following twelfth of July, effortlessly raising his voice to a shout to cover the snorts of derision coming from his opposite numbers led by councillor Doherty whose hands gripped his own proposal for a St. Patrick's Day ceilidh for the following March. They all jumped when a particularly vicious gust of wind coincided with the loss of electricity in the town, which left them isolated in the glowering morning light, face to face in their animosity.

The steadily increasing storm drove both the snow and the townsfolk into pubs, cafes and doorways, where according to temperament or fortune they either entered, or halted in the endlessly trailing progression of already hard lives, they went on, stooping, and tightening their mouths against this latest obstacle.

Emerging from the tiny library closeted underneath the town-hall, and gasping at the coldness of the day, Emer O'Rahill who had spent her morning illicitly reading in a quiet corner, of a time of honour and truthfulness which did not correspond with her day to day life, dreaded the return to reality and the daily grind. An un-noticeable woman in her thirties who generally looked older that she was, Emer had endured her years of married life by discovering a hidden passion for reading. She looked up at the huge ply-wood facsimile of the ancient Ulster hero Cuchulainn who shared the crowded doorway with her and a pitifully small banner proclaiming the legend 'Heroes of Ireland'. She spoke softly to the noble face whose eyes gazed inland toward the stone circle at Cuilbane and sighing, pulled on her headscarf and decided to wait for a few minutes to see if the storm would ease a little. Unaware that above her a fist-fight had broken out among the elected councillors of Portstewart over who should hold the town halls' one remaining candle, Emer thought the building to be standing up less well than usual to the winter weather, as bangs and crashes shook the ceiling over her head. While looking up, fearful that the building was about to fall down around her, a large pillar of black cloud above the headland to her right, caught her eye.

In fact, from Hawks Hollow on Benbane Head to the five-stone circle at Cuilbane on the upper reaches of the river Bann, some thirty kilometres inland, an enormous triangle of dark cloud was forming; its third side angled coast-ward, joining at the point where a dreaming rotunda sat on a cliffs' edge.

In the town hall committee room things were just as ominous.

Councillor Doherty and his men having staunchly defended the portals of the building had fled, leaving a not insignificant spillage of blood behind them. As Councillor Leeson blooded the uninitiated council members in the 'blood of Fenians smited by true Orange men' he was only too aware that councillor Doherty would be rounding up the local Catholic flying squad, which consisted of many and varied unemployed men of the town who were in fact secretly drilled in the parochial hall on a Wednesday night, after the weekly whist drive, by the parish priest Fr. Pearse. Even so, a quick glance outside told him that the time for a rallying call to the local Protestant equally unemployed militia was urgently required. Councillor Doherty had indeed wasted no time in gathering his troops. Having sent his battered councilmen to uncover the arms hidden in the foreign missions box behind the altar of St. Martyr's the local chapel, he had taken up his post in the preordained bunker which also doubled as the towns' bandstand during the summer tourist season. A lonely spot even in mid-August, it safely concealed both rations (soda bread, vacuum packed) and insignia (badges bearing shamrocks rampant). There he waited, frozen but determined as his ragged band of defenders joined him in dribs and drabs. At the far end of the sea-front Councillor Leeson's troops were dug in and waiting. Each man having collected his artillery from the little flower arranging vestibule in the Orange hall and proceeded post-haste to the fish-seller's stall at the harbour, where he received his ration (two mushroom vol-au-vents) and his insignia (a button-hole of fresh orange lilies).

As at either end of the storm besieged town, oaths were sworn and battle-field commissions instantly granted, Emer O'Rahill realised that she was no longer alone in the doorway of the library. Flattened against the far wall she gaped, open mouthed at the apparition before her. Standing six feet six in his goat-skin sandals, and carrying his fearsome magical club, the gae bolga, stood Cuchulainn, the legendary Hound of Ulster. In a booming voice which painfully pressed Emer's ear-drums inward he demanded of her, 'Who had summoned me from my deep slumber, to Irelands' aid?'

Caught in a time-slide from which she could barely remember calling on the spirit of the hero to come to her aid, Emer did however remember her reason for doing so, only it did not involve the ancient art of cudgel-bashing at all. Emer had need of another ancient skill; one more biblical than martial. Smoothly gripping his club, she crooned to him in the way of the ancient Irish women she had read so much about.

Hidden in the rapidly advancing swirls of black cloud, Cuchulainn's army of ancient warriors faltered in their triangular battle-formation. Sensing a drain on the life-force of their chief, the hordes of the Fianna, fearing that the battle had begun with out them, broke into a run. Inland at Cuilbane, the stone circle began to pulse with a life of its own.

As the storm reached its climax, the Fianna reached the sea front, just in time to hear the voice of their beloved chieftain pitched against the vortex of the winds crying. 'God...Yes...For Ireland.'

Misunderstanding the emotion in his words, the faithful warriors looked about for an enemy to rout. Unfortunately for the councilmen of Portstewart and their troops everyone else was sheltering inside from the weather. The Fianna bared their cudgels and fell snarling on the bandstand and the fish-seller's stall.

By the time Emer had finished with Cuchulainn he had little life-force left. The burial ground at Cuilbane was calling strongly to him. Emer, satiated, gazed dreamily as his retreating form was joined by other, strangely familiar forms. The Fianna in respect for their enemies, who had fought neither well nor bravely, were taking the bodies to rest with them at Cuilbane, until Ireland called again.

The following July, Emer sat outside the new community hall listening to the music from the Cross-community dance that was being held inside. Portstewart had benefited from losing its council members as the town had now been twinned with Hamelin in Germany, and had received a tear fund from their new sibling to compensate for the disastrous storm of the previous year.

Emer, however was much more interested in her darling first-born child and the warlike way in which his tiny little fists could manipulate his rattle.

The Gala

by

Francis Milligan

Hawkeye studied his reflection in the full length mirror. Turning to admire the cut of his new fawn coloured suit, emboldened by a Prince of Wales check, he considered the merits of growing a moustache. Taking time to adjust his cravat Hawkeye carelessly hummed that asinine tune, half remembered from some music-hall act. Being finally satisfied with this sartorial elegance, and filled by cheerful expectation, he descended the broad staircase.

On entering the dining-room Hawkeye was somewhat nonplused to find it silent and empty. Being the eldest he considered it his perogative to be last at the table, but always before The Parent. Saturday breakfasts, normally accompanied by the raucous merriment of his younger brother and sisters, had an almost festive atmosphere. Pensively surveying the table with only two places set, he recalled how Tony had taken the girls to Aunt Elaine's for the weekend.

He seated himself to the right of the imposing carving chair at the head of the table. The Parent would, with no little irascibility, exercise control of her errant brood from this dominating position. Helping himself to bacon, eggs, tomato and mushrooms from the large silver salver he wondered as to The Parent's humour. There would be nothing to distract her attentions from himself and this could lead to some unwanted scrutiny of his behaviour.

At this juncture his thoughts were interrupted by Bridie's arrival bearing a rack of toast and a pot of tea on a linen covered tray.

'Good mornin' Master William, and sure 'tis a beautiful mornin,' she said placing the toast in front of him. 'Will I pour the tea for ya?' she continued, fussing round him like a mother hen with a solitary chick.

'Yes please Bridie,' he said, smiling a welcome whilst reaching for a slice of hot toast.

'Did ya have a good night last night?' she enquired quizzically. 'Ya didn't get home till the small hours, ya rapscallion ya, ya what!' she exclaimed benevolently.

'A good night.' He enthused halting a fork-full of mushroom and bacon on route to it's destination. 'Never a night like it Bridie!' he continued setting down the fork. 'We started off in the Oxford and I didn't lose a frame. Even mis-hit

116

shots found the pockets and when that happens you have to ride your luck. I made quite a tidy packet.' He said demonstratively tapping his breast pocket. 'Don't tell the Parent though,' he continued conspiratorially before launching into a eulogy of the remainder of that dissolute night.

This flowing monologue was abruptly halted by the entrance of the imposing figure of the Parent who no doubt, with - jaundiced eye, would view such pleasure as signs of his debility.

Her *'Good morning William'* intimated that she considered ten forty-five too late in the day to be taking breakfast.

'A delightful morning Mother,' he rejoined breezily. 'This bacon's good! Have you changed your grocer?'

'Distainfully ignoring this fatuous remark and addressing the maid sternly. 'Is the tea fresh Bridie?'

'Oi've only brought the pot ta the table dis minite Ma'am, and poured a cup for Master William.'

'Don't call him Master William,' she said irritably. 'He's over twenty-one and should be addressed as Mister William.'

'Sorry Ma'am.' Bridie responded with a bobbed curtsey. 'But Oi've bin in your service dese twenty-six years, and he's Master William ta me Ma'am,' she said defiantly. 'But oi'll try to remember in future Ma'am.'

'Very well Bridie, leave the tea, I shall ring if I need anything further.'

The Parent settled in her accustomed place, as William having disposed of the last of his bacon reached for the toast.

'And what, may I enquire, are your plans for the rest of the day.' Her tone of voice intended to strike fear in the breast of her malcontent son.

'Well, I had thought of going to the meeting at Down Royal this afternoon,' he said provocatively, impervious to the threatening tone. Impishly he continued. 'But knowing your views on the racing fraternity, and having no desire to cause displeasure, I have decided to go to the swimming gala at Pickie' he concluded anticipating a favourable reaction.

William was well aware of the Parent's distaste for gambling, and unfortunately, horse racing was not included in her extensive list of healthy out-door pursuits. She much preferred activities in which one expended vast amounts of energy, there-by rendering oneself incapable of the more pleasurable dalliances of the evening.

He sensed her deprecation change to warm maternal approval on revealing his intention to participate in the diving competition.

A rain coat, draped cloak like around his shoulders, he ventured forth. The malacca cane sounding on the hard, hot pavement like the single beat of a marching drum, he proceeded to Queen's Quay Station by way of Botanic Avenue, Donegall Pass and Oxford Street, crossing the Queen's Bridge at five minutes to midday. Having purchased his ticket at precisely twelve o'clock - the noon train, invariably late in its departure - he ambled towards the platform.

From his seat by the window Hawkeye casually surveyed the last of the passengers scurrying to the carriages, his mind clinically considering the competition to come. The train pulled laboriously out of the station past the tall skeletal gantries of the shipyard and the tiny terraces housing it's workers. Picking up speed the carriage took on a comfortable regular rolling motion, which combined with the steady clickty-clack of wheels over rail joints created a soporific cocoon for Hawkeye's reverie.

Awakening in the comparative darkness of Bangor station, Hawkeye alighted from the carriage and sauntered nonchalantly to the ticket barrier. With a breezy 'Good afternoon' to the ticket collector he passed from the cool darkness of the station to searing summer sunlight.

Making his way down High Street, jostled by bustling crowds of Saturday shoppers, holiday makers and trippers down from Belfast for the day, he came into view of the bay; sparkling like millions of diamonds the surface scattered carelessly with rowing boats. Young men pulling lustily on oars, a female companion perched demurely in the stern, some of whom appeared more interested in the fashions and flirtations on the promenade wall than the exertions of their oarsmen enervated by the rays of a sun passing it's zenith.

On reaching the bottom of High Street and turning left along the Promenade every inch of the sea wall was occupied by young men, and girls wearing dresses of every conceivable hue, flirting, flitting like multi-coloured butterflies searching for nectar. Behind them wavelets sparkling and dancing reflecting their abandon. Opposite, cafes' and shops' clamorous with customers. Children, some in sailor suits, buying sweets and ice-cream; squealing in delight, others, in tears, and screams of frustration as fraught parents denied their incessant pleas.

Progressing at a leisurely pace through this heaving mass of vibrant humanity, Hawkeye could see the steep rows of spectators surrounding Pickie Pool. The raucous applause, on the completion of a race, clearly discernible above the clamour surrounding him, set his adrenalin flowing.

118

As Hawkeye was ushered through the entrance reserved for competitors the tumultuous applause for the victor in the final swimming race erupted, a drawn-out joyous baying reminiscent of a pack of hounds in full flight in sight of quarry. Not one to miss the opportunity he timed his appearance to perfection. The cheers barely dead in their throats, he stepped forward and bowed deeply from the waist to either side. A palpable expectancy gripped the galleries as he strolled to the poolside, nonchalantly twirling the malacca cane, the coat flowing back from his shoulders like a full sail before the wind. His friends set up the shout 'Hawkeye, Hawkeye.' The crowd taking their lead, enhanced the cry with a rhythmic, palpitating hand clap. He responded to this adulation by dancing a little two-step shuffle and raising the cane in both hands high above his head. In a final, mocking obeisance Hawkeye lost his footing causing his untimely propulsion to the centre of the pool.

To the accompaniment of the unmitigated merriment of the gallery he sank to the bottom. His body, with head tucked, was indiscernible, beneath the billowing coat, to those above.

The rain coat rose, buoyed by a pocket of air, when Hawkeye released the button at his throat. Transfixed by the grotesque inert shape, distorted by refraction, a tremulous murmur swept through the audience. The body floated gently upwards.

Hawkeye, covered by his coat, had unsheathed the sword in the cane. On regaining the surface he rolled onto his back and thrust the naked blade aloft! The gallery, as one, came to it's feet with a tumultuous roar of approval believing this to be the much advertised novelty act.

Till Death Us Do Part

by

Michael Withers

Harry Richards glowered at the computer screen. He was trying to start his latest novel, but his brain wouldn't work. This was unusual, since he had found that his methodical life usually produced lots of ideas.

He rose each morning at seven, had his shower and breakfast, helped his wife with their three children, and then walked with them to their local primary school. He was at his desk promptly at 9am. There was no phone in the room. The desk faced into a corner so that he would not be distracted by anything in the garden. At 12.30pm he came out, had lunch, watched the one o'clock news, went for a walk, and sat down at his desk by 2pm.

At 4.30pm on the dot there would be a sound of scuffling outside the door. It would burst open as the children poured in, followed by Janet who carried a tray with afternoon tea. They had tea together, and then Harry played with the children until their evening meal was ready.

After the children had gone to bed, if neither had a nightclass to take, they would read, listen to music, or watch TV.

Janet was a qualified Home Economics teacher, but Harry had persuaded her to give up her work when they had started a family. Last autumn, without asking him, she had agreed to teach an evening class. He had been furious at first, but later had come round, even to the extent of encouraging her to go for a drink after teaching with some of her pupils.

Harry had met his wife twelve years ago at the nightclass he taught. She had come into the room wearing a pair of tight-fitting trousers and sweater, with her ginger hair flowing free. He had felt his stomach lurch and he knew that he had to have her, no matter what the cost. They had married within a year, and everything had gone perfectly well. His writing had gone from success to success and had enabled him to buy a beautiful old house. They had been effortlessly blessed with three healthy children. Everyone knew how lucky he was.

As he glared at the screen, there was a knock on the door. He swivelled round in his chair angry for a moment at being interrupted, but remembered that Janet would only disturb him in an emergency. The door opened, and she came in, pale, frail, and very ill at ease.

He started to say: 'What's wrong love?' when he saw that a man was following her into the room. He was tall like Harry but heavier built. Though wearing a suit, he had the outdoor look of a labouring man.

Janet took a couple of quick breaths: 'This is Gordon. I'm going to live with him.' Her legs gave under her, and she sat down in an armchair.

Harry was visibly stunned, his mouth dropped open, his eyes widened, and there was silence for a few moments. Then he took a deep breath and said 'I don't know what to say. How long has this been going on?'

As Janet seemed incapable of answer, Gordon replied: 'About six months. We met at Janet's nightclass. My wife died and I thought that I had better learn to look after myself.'

Harry nodded in glazed comprehension, and turned to Janet: 'But what about us: our love, all the good times, all that we've created together? Doesn't that count for anything?'

Janet said nothing, but bowed her head and held out her hand to Gordon for comfort.

'What about our wedding vows; 'Till death us do part'?'

Janet bowed her head even further, and her hand in Gordon's trembled visibly.

'And what about the children? You know what all the reports say about the harm a broken marriage causes children. Is your 'love' worth such a price?'

Still no word came from the bowed head, but her other hand reached up to hold Gordon's hand even more firmly. For his part, Gordon stood on guard at her side, with his left hand on her shoulder, indicating possession.

Harry sat for a long time with his head in his hands, and then gave a deep sigh: 'OK. You wouldn't have come to me if your minds weren't made up, so let's do this like sensible, mature people. The first thing to do is to make this official for us, by returning our wedding rings. I must say I never thought that I'd be taking mine off in this world.'

As Harry struggled to get his ring off, he thought of the happiness of their wedding, the birth of their children, the many, many good times they had together. Then he crossed the room and swopped rings with Janet.

'Now what about the children?' he asked.

'I think,' said Janet in a low voice, 'that children are better off with the mother. Though of course I'll be glad for you, I'll *want* you, to have access to the children. They love you.'

'Access,' said Gordon 'at any *reasonable* hour.'

'It *will* work out Harry, you'll see,' said Janet looking up at Gordon obviously slightly cross with him.

'Yes, that's probably the best course.'

'What about money and property?' Gordon wanted to know.

Harry gave him a filthy look before looking at Janet: 'I've always regarded us as a team - fifty/fifty. So I'll have a word with Bill Ferguson telling him what I want, and you get your solicitor to contact him. It will be all done fairly. There's one thing I think that I have the right to ask of you. When you're talking to our parents, tell them exactly what happened. Don't bad mouth me.'

Janet nodded in silent agreement, wondering how on earth she could break the news to both sets of parents.

Harry went on: 'When do you intend leaving?'

Gordon answered: 'We're going round now to hire a van. We don't need to move any heavy stuff, just Janet's personal belongings and the children's things.'

With that he helped Janet to her feet, and they went out the door, with Janet barely able to walk.

Harry looked out of his study window. Beside his new Merc, was this pathetic mini. He thought Gordon had done well when he had caught the attention of the wife of a successful writer. The dog came barking out of the house and Harry wryly observed how it jumped into the back seat, just as though it was used to doing it. They drove out the gate and out of sight. Harry stood, fingering Janet's wedding ring, and waited to see if she would change her mind and come back.

When she didn't he walked into the kitchen, picked up the phone and dialled. When someone answered he said: 'Hello Darling, I thought you'd like to know 'Romeo and Juliet' have just been to tell me of their affair. Did they think I was blind? I thought they would never pluck up the courage. God! she's no taste. Hmm? Yes, everything's settled. They think they're getting half of my possessions, the silly fools. Hmmm? No, I don't think it would be wise for you to come round for a while. We'll go on as we've been doing this past year. Hmmm? Oh yes I'll be at the class to-night as usual, and *afterwards,* if you've nothing on. Especially if you've *nothing* on! Hmmm? Yes, I love you too, my darling. 'Bye.'

The Duster

by

Margaret Cameron

The nasturtiums spilling over the hanging basket outside the french windows began to stir in the soft morning breeze; an indication the promised weather forecast was proving correct. Friday had been a day of showers but the overnight strong wind had chased the rain clouds away. The Saturday forecast - warm and dry with clear sunny spells and light winds - would be ideal.

Cynthia Berryman had been paying particular attention to the forecast for the weekend, especially for Saturday. Since her twin sons had gone to Boarding School she had time to involve herself in a number of Groups and Committees. She was just the type of person gladly welcomed to carry out such duties as Secretary, Treasurer or Chairwoman.

As Chairwoman of the Fund Raising Committee for resurfacing the local tennis courts, she thought it but right that she should entertain the Honorary President of the Club and his wife for a barbecue lunch on the Saturday. She would update her guests on the future fund raising plans with a view to a donation. She secretly smiled at her thoughts and plans.

'Housewifes could do so much in the community,' she often remarked when her less interested neighbours declined to become involved in any of her projects. Some neighbours regarded her as toffy nosed with grandiose ideas and of being a name dropper, but Mrs Berryman didn't see her self in that way.

'I'm on good terms with all my neighbours but I don't believe in running in and out of each others houses,' she said in her self justified manner.

The neighbours held the family in high esteem and smiled politely when Mrs Berryman was spoken of. Mr Berryman was an agreeable man who avoided any disharmony. More approachable than his wife he was very popular with the neighbours, young and old. The children found him a friend when their bicycles broke down. The less mechanically minded husbands relied upon his advice and help when the radiators leaked or the TV picture slipped. David Berryman was an all round handyman they said.

'David, the rain yesterday has spoilt the windows. Could you clean the lounge window quickly before they come?'

123

'Yeah, in a minute,' came the muffled voice through the grey billowing smoke from the barbecue.

'Do it now David. They are due here soon.'

She was pleased when David picked up the cleaning pail with its collection of dusters and cleaning fluid and started the window so promptly. The windolene brought a pink flush to the face of the window pane as he applied the cloth in a circular movement. Mrs Berryman was always motivated by other people working. She bustled around the kitchen and stopped to turn the steaks marinating in the sauce. Everything was going to plan and well timed. She tasted the salad dressing, savouring the flavour like a connoisseur and then added more seasoning.

Voices outside made her look out. David was giving the window a final polish and was talking to someone. She wished he would hurry up. Then Barry and Maud, from two houses up, came into view. Oh no, she thought, they will only keep him talking. They must still be having problems with papering that room, why don't they get it done professionally. She felt impatient with her neighbours.

David continued polishing the window pane but at intervals stopped to make some point in the conversation. When he stopped he shook out the polishing duster and changed its position in his hand. It was when he gave the duster a further flap that Mrs Berryman recognised it.

She stood at the french windows looking across the lounge helpless and feeling more and more humiliated. David, oblivious of his wife or duster, continued to chat and every now and again gave it another shake out. Before she could decide how to get her husband indoors, the white Porche swung into the driveway.

Mrs Berryman groaned - if only she had cut them up in pieces or taken out the elastic. It was bad enough to have Barry and Maud see them but the President and his wife seeing her knickers being used as a duster - she was mortified. Wait till she got him in.

A Small Disintegration

by

Peter Hough

There was no breath of air to stir the pall of yellow grey smoke that hung like a conscience, over the street. Every chimney added to the murk and the yellow sodium lamps only made strange haloes in it. The smoke was cloying, sweet smelling and peaty; redolent of hearth and home, the very essence of an Ireland that had ceased to exist when people moved out of holes in the ground and into rude hovels. Winter dusk in the North of Ireland. The smoke struggled up and out of the chimneys to fall back to the ground, like water from a frozen fountain. Down at the shore, the tide was in. White and grey birds rode the greasy swells, their plumage catching the glare of headlights and Christmas illuminations. The birds bobbed amongst the beer cans and carrier bags that remained attached to the shore, fixed by invisible strands of elastic. Young people shouted and laughed on the Promenade. Their breath plumed like the smoke from the chimneys. Winter dusk in the North of Ireland. Children were getting ready for bed and men were sitting down to meat and potatoes. Up and down the cold street, curtains were being pulled across the windows.

From my eyrie at the top of the house I could survey all around. I could see the lights twinkling in Donegal, I could see disembodied hands in Marigold gloves washing up in the kitchen next door. I liked to sit in the gathering gloom with a mug of hot, sweet tea and my gas fire on to take away the chill of the evening air. Up there I wrote, up there I fanned the sparks of my imagination and hoped that great conflagrations would result. There had been no bonfires of stunning original thought for sometime, up there. From this perch I could see all around and not be seen myself. Seen or observed, watched or noticed. The communication mast behind the RUC station worried me. There was just too much I didn't know. This was not my place.

It was some time since the sun had slipped gracefully out of view somewhere behind Castlerock. Above the sky was a deep royal blue and pocked with stars a sliver of moon hung like a mystical symbol embroidered onto a magician's robe. Everything was serene and mysterious up there. Down below, life was gritty and smoky. Life and death. What was one without the other? One could not exist alone. I often considered my own death yet rarely contemplated my

125

own life. I could not bear to linger in pain, or watch myself deteriorating, I did not want to become a burden. Falling from a high place would have been my preferred method of release. The red light on top of the communication mast was on. They were watching me again.

My own place was not this place. That was why they were watching me. My place was warmer, softer. In my place people were distant and aloof, inland people, miles from the sea and calm like lakes and rivers. But roots were only for holding people down. Mine were always near the surface, easy to pull up and set down somewhere else. The 'hows' and 'whys' of my peregrinations were not things that I like to discuss. I got around, as they say. Whatever I did, I always had one eye looking inward. Mostly life was unsatisfactory; it was not my fault. I was only a victim of circumstance. My life had careered from incident to incident, only some of which were real. That damned red light was winking again. Something bad was going to happen.

A car detached itself from the flow of traffic on the main road and entered our street. It was neither the McCreadys nor Mr Crawford from next door. It was not Mrs Connolly from Lisburn who came up on Fridays to visit her mother in the houses opposite. It was not the potato sellers or the students who lodged up the road. A surge of nervous energy coursed through me. Whatever was happening, was happening now and I would watch it all from up here in my dark eyrie. The car stopped almost opposite the house and I could see a trickle of exhaust smoke as the engine was left running. What sort of car was it? It might be important to know. There were two in the car, well, four knees that I could see. What were they doing? One was holding a book open. This was intriguing. I just knew that they were coming to my house. And I knew why. It didn't have to be me, but it might as well be I had never sought to hide the fact that I was English. I had never shouted about it either. Diplomatic me. However, British I was, white Protestant male. I had done the alternative tourist trip up the Falls in the car and had been fascinated and repelled. Hundreds of yards of newsreels whirred through my head. Big media Brother had been force feeding me too long and now, in the smoky dusk in the North of Ireland, I was about to become a statistic. And I had never even offered an opinion. The car door opened.

He had the leather jacket, little moustache, and he vaulted our low wall and disappeared under the porch roof. I was ready for it but even so, the doorbell made me leap like a Bann salmon. If I sat up here in the dark, would he go away? Would he sledgehammer the door down and find me? I had to answer that doorbell. I thought of my Mother as I went down the steps. I am not brave,

126

but I believe in fate. I relished every breath, the feel of the carpet under my feet. He stood framed in the glass of the door, distorted and anonymous.

I opened the door and looked him right in the eye. His hand went into his inside pocket. This was it. He spoke.

'Milk money.'

'What?' Some macabre joke, surely. His hand came out of his pocket holding a notebook. He glanced at it.

'Two pounds thirty one, please.'

'Oh, milk money' blushing to the roots of my hair I paid the man. He smiled.

'Thank you. Cheerio now!'

'Bye then.' I closed the door on the smoky near darkness, and laughed.

Endings and Beginnings

by

J C Nelson

Joy stood staring down at the Obituary notice in the Belfast Telegraph. As unbidden tears welled up in her deep brown eyes and began to flow unchecked down her cheeks, she stood still in her Peter Storm jacket not at all mindful that on her way back from the paper shop she had been splashed and soaked by a passing lorry and that drips were cascading down onto her living room carpet. Her dog, pawing at her legs roused her momentarily and she unclipped his lead but instead of placing in on its accustomed hook in the hall, she let it drop, brown and dead on the floor.

Heading for the kitchen to fetch a towel to dry the dog she passed the Drinks Cabinet and paused briefly. 'No - I don't want to dilute this pain,' she thought as she proceeded. 'I have to face this one by myself.'

Sinking into her accustomed end of the settee two minutes later, she lifted up the Tele again to reread the notice and as she did, her thoughts were transferred from suburban Lambeg 1988 to Lurgan Co Armagh nearly thirty years before.

They were a motley crew, those assembled in J.I.III at Lurgan College, the clever ones who would 'sit' the Junior in three years unlike their contemporaries the non-qualifiers of J.I. IV. Amongst all the newcomers were two girls who had attended the Prep School and who felt just a little smug as they knew their way around. It took them only a few days to realise how little Prep School had helped advance the cause of Algebra and Geometry while the basics of both had been competently tackled by the contributory Primary School teachers.

There they all stood, the girls in their navy blue box pleated gym tunics, red and navy girdles neatly knotted round thin and fat waists alike, white blouses, red and navy ties and navy blazers with the owl emblazoned on the pocket. They were self-conscious as were the boys in their mainly short grey trousers, navy blazers white shirts and heavy grey knee socks. Stout black brogues encased male and female feet alike.

As the soft Indian summer which always seemed to linger in September gave way finally to the first crisp mornings of October with just a nip in the air, and the cobwebs in the hedges began to appear every morning, friendship began to

128

dissolve, form and regroup. All the girls with the exception of one hailed from the immediate area, Dollingstown, Maralin, Moira, Donacloney and Lurgan itself, or at least they had lived there for sometime. There was one new girl. She had lived in Newcastle until, in the August of that year, her father's work had necessitated a move. Her name was Maureen and she wore a bra! Towards her, the rest of the girls, though cordial, were wary. They would observe her as she strained to climb one of the giant oak trees, her pointed nipples effortlessly pointing heavenward, as they in their vests and camisoles stood admiringly and at the same time aloof. Oh what became of you, Maureen of the bra? Do you remember too the small slice of life that was shared all those years ago?

There were the farmers' daughters from Maralin - heavy conscientious country girls who always seemed to have the right answers to algebraic problems and who smugly protected their homework books early in the morning, and shook pious heads at other less righteous seekers after correctness. These girls were the teachers' pets. Their hands shot up failingly for Mademoiselle. Their books were never blotted or lost or torn. They were the paragons.

There were also two girls who first smiled at each other, made polite remarks and speedily became friends. Neither was able afterwards to pin-point the first meeting or the first words. Like most significant moments in life it must have come unheralded and passed unnoticed. Yet soon a veritable twosome was formed - the quick moving tall fair girl with piercing blue eyes and skinny legs and her slower, stouter, dark-haired, dark eyed companion had recognised a 'Je ne sais quoi' in each other and that was that!

Oh those frosty bicycle rides to school that first winter, pedalling eagerly and carelessly until the treacherous icy roads warned them after many skids to slow down. And oh, the scent of early Summer mornings, when Joy would cycle down the Gilford Road, meet Lucy at the corner and their blue and white gingham dresses blowing in the Summer breeze, giggle and exchange secrets along Union Street, through the town and down the Lough Road to face the challenge of Latin declensions and French verbs with Winkibow and Mademoiselle, undaunted.

Saturdays were Saturdays in those days! Household chores completed, bedroom finally tidied, Joy would race down from Toberhuney Lane to the Banbridge Road early in the afternoon. Sometimes the friends strolled into the town to change library books and enjoy the highlight of the day, a visit to Cafollas for a marshmallow ice-cream. Then back to Lucy's house they sped for High Tea. 'Dixon of Dock Green' gave way to 'The Black and White Minstrels'

strels' and this was the signal that Saturday was, for all intents and purposes over, that week.

The Summer the Everly Brothers hit Lurgan many a Saturday afternoon was spent under a huge beech tree in Lucy's front garden, while the two and Pat, Lucy's younger sister tried to form themselves into the equivalent female group. Joy directed and bossed the other two whose musical talent was limited but all the exhortations to 'do it properly - no laughing' ended in the same way with giggles, shouts and scuffles.

Another Summer the Sunday School outing to Newcastle became an important date in the girls' calendar. Lucy even joined the Sunday School so that she would be permitted to attend. How they loved that train journey, the race along the sands, the sandy sandwiches, the melting lollies, the first giggling exchanges with boys and how they wished the bumpy journey back would never end. Best of all perhaps was the mulling over all the events on the Monday morning as they stood casually at the locker area, near to the Prefects' Room where the gods that year resided. Nothing ever happened but that did not matter. The buzz was what kept them alert, keen, ready to face each day as though something special would happen. Someone would recognise a greatness, a soulmate in either teenage girl some day...

The only tragedy which befell them shocked the entire school. Buddy Holly, the Peggy Sue hiccuper died and for one morning the school was silent. Sobs could be heard from behind raised desk lids and 'Lettres de Mon Moulin' and 'Everyday Life in Rome' received scant attention. A genius had died. Yet, with the resilience and insulation of youth, the grief soon passed and 'Jail House Rock' began to reverberate down the corridor from the Sixth Form Room. Joy and Lucy stood at the locker area a lot, enviously regarding the closed door. How many more years would pass before they too could enter its hallowed portals?

Sharply and suddenly Joy was brought back to the present by the nearly simultaneous ringing of her front door bell and the accompanying bark from her Border Collie dog. Having greeted, paid the coalman and commented on the weather, automatically she reclaimed her seat by the fire.

'If only I had known,' she mused. 'She might have been in Beaconsfield while I was visiting there last Summer. I could have passed her as I did so many with eyes quickly averted, not wanting to see anymore suffering than was necessary. Would I have recognised her? Would she have recognised me?'

Jumping up she strode swiftly towards the hall and regarded herself critically in the mirror. A white oval shaped face surrounded by a mass of dark brown curly hair was reflected there. The eyes looked dark and puffy and somehow her lips quivered as though she was not quite in control.

She remembered the only time she had ever seen Lucy lose control. As she arrived one Saturday afternoon she had heard through the open window, a loud angry voice interspersed with choking sob. 'I've no clothes at all. I can't go out. Nothing fits me. Look at Joy - she's got a new skirt and blouse. Nobody ever thinks about me...!

Joy remembered Lucy's mother's tired tired blue eyes as they had regarded her daughter and her daughter's friend in turn before she spoke.

'You can both go into the Tweedy Acheson's this afternoon and Lucy, you can choose a skirt and blouse. Put the bill on my account.'

Joy's blouse was yellow, a bright yellow and it had half sleeves. Later that afternoon Lucy was also wearing a yellow blouse, but hers was a sharp, acidy yellow and had capped sleeves. Days afterwards both girls agreed that the perfect blouse would have capped sleeves but be the colour of Joy's.

The only other time both girls had been upset had been in the Summer of the year they sat for the 'Junior'. Joy's father who was in the RUC was being transferred yet again and this time to Ballymena. Bitter tears were shed and protestations of everlasting friendship were made before Joy left Lucy clutching in her arms her friend's parting gift - Buddy Holly's 'Raining in my Heart' and the Everly Brothers 'Bird Dog'.

Many letters winged their way between Ballymena and Lurgan throughout August, September and October of that year, until Hallowe'en when Joy went to spend half term with Lucy. Yet already a slight change, not obvious then, but evident enough looking back, was there. Joy, unhappy at a different school, had somehow passed out of the old circle and no longer seemed to quite belong. No more visits were made and letters became less frequent and eventually ceased. Yet many a time, throughout the years that passed, Joy at the back of her mind clung to the idea that someday she and Lucy would meet up again. It never occurred to her as she settled into adult life, well established in her chosen career, that some endings, like beginnings are unexpected and unrecognisable at the time.

Her mother's phone call at 6.00 that March evening had came as no surprise. But the words had.

'Joy, I've just been looking at the paper. I'm afraid I've some bad news for you - Lucy...'

131

Joy had gulped back the tears. She had slammed down the receiver, grabbed her jacket, lead and dog and burst out unheedingly into the dark, stormy evening to get the proof - to see with her own eyes what she had been told was true. Now as she again stared at the Obituary Notice, random escapist thoughts sped through her whirling brain.

'That's not her name - it's a mistake - no of course. She must have married. Fancy, Lucy married and I never knew. That couldn't be right. Children? Lucy couldn't have had children without me knowing? How could this be?'

Lucy was more with Joy during the months that followed than she had been for most of the years since they had been separated. 'If only,' she often thought and then as time passed and the first wild grief became more accepting, she tried to rationalise this.

'If only what? - if only her father had not been transferred - that wouldn't have changed the end result - if only she had remained friends, attended the wedding, known the children, could something more have been done - who knows? What guarantee was there that the friendship would have lasted throughout the rest of their school days and later college days?'

'The one sure thing in life is that nothing remains the same,' she reminded herself. 'Those two eleven year old girls who first met all those years ago are both dead. Those two bosom pals who went everywhere together, talked endlessly and who never tired of each other's company belong to the past, not even a shared past anymore. So it is as though they both never existed.'

What if they had known that one would like this after 'Long suffering courageously borne!' That would have changed nothing - those bright blue and yellow days of youth would have dismissed such notions as morbid. They knew they would live forever and soon the air would have been filled again with peals of girlish laughter...

Which World

by

Margaret Partridge

The gentle waves of the rose-coloured sea lapped at the silver sand. The blue leaves of the trees that fringed the cove whispered an accompaniment to the waves, and the girl who stood on the deserted beach complimented the alien beauty around her. She stood motionless as a statue held in wonderment by the magical quality of her surroundings. The warmth of the sand beneath her feet tempted her gaze away from the incredible flora, and looking down she saw myriads of jewel-like flecks interspersed through the silver grains.

'But they can't be jewels,' she whispered in awe. 'Jewels are hard and cold.' Faith had never seen such loveliness, even in her dreams.

Acting on a sudden urge to touch the rose crystal waves, she moved towards the water's edge. Looking down into the soft ripples, her eyes opened wide in amazement and disbelief.

The reflection that gazed back at her was of a young girl. Golden tendrils of hair caressed the fragile pre-Raphaelite face as the gentle breeze stirred the warm air.

'No, it can't be,' she stammered. 'I'm old - so very old. Once, many years ago I looked like that, but not now.'

'And why not?' said a quiet voice behind her.

She stopped sobbing abruptly and turned to face the tall handsome man who stood smiling at her. For some strange reason Faith wasn't surprised at his very sudden but silent appearance. Somehow, his being there completed the haunting dream-like quality of her surroundings.

'Why not, you say. Well I'll tell you why not.' She took a deep breath. 'I've lived a many many years now, and I'm tired. Life's not been too kind, and that reflection recalled memories I'd just sooner forget.' Her quiet indignation slowly evaporated before the calmness and serenity of his face. 'Don't think I'm ungrateful for the good I have known, but the pain of living has become more than I can bear. Last night I thought my pain would soon be over and I thought it was, until I saw that vision of myself in the sea.' She sighed deeply. 'That was how I looked when I married my Samuel.'

Turning to the delicate transparent purity of the rose sea she whispered to herself, 'Any minute now Faith Peplow you'll wake up in your hospital bed. This dream will be gone and it'll be the start of another long long day.'

Feeling a gentle touch on her arm she turned again to face the stranger.

'No it won't Faith Peplow - this is not a dream you're experiencing. This is real life, the world that is never far away.' His words were spoken with a deep conviction. 'Forget the pain. It has no place here. You will not age anymore neither will you weep, except maybe tears of joy.' Holding out his hand to her, he went on. 'And there is much joy for you here. Come with me, and let me show you some of the wonders of this world.'

Reaching out she confidently put her slim hand in his, and felt a great assurance grow within her as side by side they started to walk up the gentle incline that led from the seashore to the blue trees fringing the bay.

If this is a dream let it go on she thought, as she felt the surge and excitement of youth pounding through her body. But this is more than a dream - it has to be.

The man led Faith through tiny picturesque hamlets that echoed a fond recall of summer memories and contented days of her young girlhood. Samuel, her first and only love had courted her in a similar village to the ones they were now passing through. She saw great cities that towered in magnificent splendour, bringing to her mind some of the ancient wonders of the world that she had read of in her school books many years ago. The greatest wonder she saw though, were the mysterious and awesome Halls of Learning.

'All the knowledge and expertise that ever was is accumulated here,' said her guide. 'The greatest works of poets, painters, writers, philosophers and scientists are all here to be studied.'

'And music too,' breathed Faith, as the soft tranquil melodies around them seemed to weave a pathway to her innermost being.

'Music above all Faith,' intoned her friend. 'Music is the language of the spheres and the universal communications. Haunting and harmonious, it is the environment of sound that supports and calms your soul.'

With these profound words held close to her heart and the quiet caress of the music streaming through her, she followed the stranger out into the wide spacious gardens.

Up to this point Faith hadn't really looked at the people who passed by, but now she began to notice their faces. And it was the peoples faces that gave her the first feelings of belonging in this intriguing and fascinating world.

Most of the faces were very familiar, she felt she had been seeing them most of her life. When a tall dreamy-eyed man passed them with a friendly nod and she recognised his face, her wonder was replaced by excitement. Trying to suppress her mounting emotions she whispered, 'That *was* William Shakespeare wasn't it?' Pausing for a few seconds to digest the enormity of what she had said she again repeated, 'That *was* William Shakespeare - I know it was.'

Her guide's smile was one of pleasure. 'Yes, you are right Faith. At last you are beginning to understand the truth of what you see.'

'But everything and everyone here are so real and substantial. The people all have a joyful vitality that is at odds with the traditional picture of 'ghosts' and 'spirits'.'

Her friend laughed with genuine amusement. 'But of course we are joyful and vital Faith. Why shouldn't we be? We have left the unreality of the Dark World behind us, and are now being constantly refreshed as the mystery and beauty of the Inner Self is revealed. I tell you girl, this world has more substance than any man could dream of.'

Leaving the restful perfection of the beautiful gardens and the elegance and splendour of the cities, once again Faith was taken to a small village, but *this* idyllic little place with it's white-washed cottages and holly-hocked gardens was immediately recognisable to her.

'Look,' she exclaimed excitedly. 'There's the school I used to go to, and the village hall where we had so many good times. Everything is exactly as it was, except for...' Her words trailed away in sudden sadness.

'Except for your loved ones,' said her friend gently. Taking her hand in his he led her to the well-remembered home of her girlhood. Standing by the weather-beaten door of the little cottage and obeying an unspoken command, she looked into the compelling blue eyes of this man who had shown her so much. The love she saw there was timeless. The understanding endless.

'You need me no longer Faith,' he said quietly. 'The love in your heart has finally brought you to your own nirvana. That which was can be again - but more so. The dreams you have dreamt your dearest aspirations, are all here waiting to be fulfilled, and the ones whose love you have so inspired are all here to share with you the timelessness of this life.'

To Faith's unspoken question he answered, 'Yes, this is what the people on Earth call Heaven, and the people you see here are called dead. There is no death in this great universe. It is just a natural transition from the cocoon of darkness to the emergence of the butterfly on a chosen bright star.'

Faith had never realised how little she knew or how much she had taken for granted in her eighteen years of life. Her whole life had been cushioned by the love and caring that had surrounded her, but now the almost unbelievable revelations of the past few hours (or was it days?) had shaken her passive acceptance of the village mores that she had grown up with.

Was this small village just a minute part of the galactic system as yet unrecognised? Was the Dark World somewhere out there amongst the other teeming millions of stars, and had she Faith Peplow, once lived a previous life on that suffering Dark World?

She would never know for sure. But as she gazed at the graceful blue-leafed tree that shaded the corner of her mother's garden, she vowed that she would search beyond the barriers of accepted doctrines and she would never again take for granted the conception of life.

Habits of a Lifetime

by

Maurice McAleese

Sometimes when he was explaining things, old Mr Smithers would use a lot of fancy words and phrases, especially if he got started on the finer points of criminal law, and I found it difficult to grasp exactly what he meant.

Mr Smithers was a retired police Inspector and he talked to me in a flattering sort of way, as if I knew as much about law enforcement procedures as himself. A lot of it was over my head, not that it mattered all that much. Mostly I just listened: a polite smile or an agreeing nod of the head was enough to keep the old man happy.

He was frail and stooped now and his hair had turned almost white but in his younger days he had been a fine figure of a man. A faded photograph in a silver frame he kept on the mantelpiece showed him standing tall and erect, as if on guard duty, and very handsome he looked, I must say.

My policy of keeping on the right side of him meant that I had to make sure his morning paper was delivered on time, no matter what the weather. And I never missed calling each week to get paid because he didn't like the bill mounting up.

A stickler for order and discipline was Mr Smithers due, I supposed, to his training as a policeman. He'd been retired for almost ten years but sometimes he acted as if he was still on the force.

'The habits of a lifetime are hard to break, lad,' he would say. 'My wife's always giving off to me but I just can't help it. Don't expect I'll ever change now.'

I had it at the back of my mind to join the police myself as soon as I was old enough, so that was another reason why I wanted to make a good impression on Mr Smithers. It would be no bad thing for a prospective recruit like myself to be able to list a former Inspector, no less, as being an old friend. No bad thing at all.

I remember how pleased he was when I informed him of my intention to join up. There and then he'd insisted on showing me his old uniform which he kept tucked away in a wardrobe in his bedroom. Proudly he laid it out on top of the bed and as he did so the preserving aroma of mothballs filled the room.

137

Mr Smithers put a restraining hand on my shoulder, as if arresting me, but it was only because he wanted me to stand back and view the hallowed uniform to the best possible advantage.

'Wait till I pull these curtains back a bit and let some more light in. Then you'll be able to see better.'

A thin shaft of dusty sunlight fell on a row of polished silver buttons and they fair sparkled as the pair of us stood gazing in silent admiration at the fine cut of the dark green jacket. A shiny brown leather belt with a smart shoulder strap attached gave an added touch of status and authority.

I felt like a million dollars when Mr Smithers invited me to try on the gold-braided Inspector's cap. It came a bit low down over my forehead but when I held my head well back I could see in the mirror that it nearly fitted me. There was also a black, silver-topped cane and the old man took great pains to show me the correct way to hold it under my arm.

He chuckled gleefully: 'We'll make a policeman out of you yet, lad. Sure you'll be an Inspector in no time. No time at all.'

I generally called to get paid for the papers on a Saturday morning because then I wasn't in such a rush as I didn't have to worry about being late for school. Mr Smithers would invite me to come in and sit down for a chat and have a cup of tea, an invitation I always accepted.

In spite of his age, he had a good memory and could recall events which had happened forty or even fifty years ago. Occasionally he would refer to his scrap-book, one of his proudest possessions. It was leather-bound and seemed to contain a complete record of his career in the police force, with old newspaper cuttings and documents recording the various important stages of his progress through the ranks.

'I like to take a wee stroll down memory lane now and again, Jamie,' he would say. 'Remind me to show it to you properly some day when you've more time.'

I never did get a good look at that old scrap-book. You see, old Mr Smithers passed away while dozing in his chair beside the fire the very next day. I was allowed to stay off school for the funeral and as I watched the slow procession making its way to the cemetery, I couldn't take my eyes off the gold-braided Inspector's cap resting proudly, but sadly, on top of the coffin.

A few days later a 'For Sale' sign went up on Mr Smithers' old house and it wasn't long before a 'sold' sticker was pasted across the sign.

Before the new owners moved in there was an auction and the auctioneer looked puzzled when I joined in the bidding for a bundle of dusty old books.

I got them for five pounds, almost all the money I had saved from my paper round. It was more than I had expected to pay, but I didn't mind. In the bundle was the faded old scrap-book Mr Smithers had been meaning to show me. I felt sure he would have wanted me to have it...

The Con Trick

by

Bert McKimm

The pretty and curvaceous little girl-woman sitting on her overstuffed sofa opposite me was working herself up into a temper. She was obviously as stubborn as I was.

I started to explain it, very patiently, all over again. The account was a large one, voluminously documented, around the five thousand mark, with a special note from some boffin in Head Office to pull out all the stops on this one. That meant Court action and a Civil Bill if necessary. Unless I could block it, of course, for no Debt Collector worth his salt or his commission has any welcome for interference from the legal eagles in a good area where he could become The Enemy overnight.

The house was neat and well-cared-for, with cherry blossoms everywhere, smart paintwork, a neat garden looking down over the distant tower-blocks of Belfast, a home that did not look as though it housed troubles or debts or worries of any sort. Which should have alerted me to smell a rat, but it didn't.

She was starting to weep a bit.

'I never owed anybody anything in my whole life,' she sobbed, 'and nobody said different.'

I'd have to ease the tension somehow. Humour always works.

'Madam,' I said, 'I'm nearly in tears myself.'

'Why?' She started to hiccup slightly.

'You're sitting on my hat.'

She jumped up and retrieved the flattened relic, suddenly giggling, and I pressed home the advantage.

'There's nothing to cry about,' I said, 'Nobody is going to hound you if I can help it, but I have a job to do like anybody else. You have admitted who you are, we have your name right, we have your correct address and we have a sheaf of evidence about the suites of furniture that were delivered to you and affidavits from carriers to prove you got them. If you had paid for the stuff in the first place I wouldn't be here. But I'm not an ogre and you have only to make a reasonable offer to settle in a reasonable time to stop us taking action I have no wish to start.'

Pull out the stops on this one, the boffin said. Lean on them hard when there are no witnesses, Sammy the One had advised me when I was new to the game. But what did they expect me to do? Put the tearful Letitia over my knee and whack her delightful contours with the rolled-up account? I confess I savoured the idea before discarding it, reluctantly.

'I'm not paying anybody anything and you can do whatever you like or whatever you damn well please!' She was weeping very noisily now, mulish and adamant.

'I'm sorry, very sorry,' I said, and was surprised to find that I meant it, and not only for the fact that it was slipping from my hands. 'Now it will go to the Court to decide. The next man to call will bring a summons.'

One of my failures. Now the legal eagles could get busy on their Civil Bill that I would have to recommend on the appropriate form. The news would spread like wildfire, and some day I would find my car sitting on four flat tyres, the standard warning to Debt Collectors to tread lightly.

I was still nursing that account and pondering how I could turn it to my benefit before surrendering it, commission-less, to the boys upstairs when I parked, a few days later, at a rural reach of the Lagan. I unscrewed my flask of coffee and settled down to see how the moorhen's numerous brood had developed since my last visit.

Another knight of the road parked alongside me and got out his flask of coffee. I wound window. 'Snap!' I said, being by nature gregarious.

We nattered and talked shop and discussed this and that and tossed it hither and yon, as one is apt to do. Real estate must have been booming, for he was well-nourished and suited.

I realised during the conversation, and mentioned in passing, that I was going to have to take one of his tenants to Court.

'Oh,' he said, 'Where?' or 'Who?' or words of that effect.

I told him about the weeping woman.

'Seems a familiar one.' He frowned in concentration. 'Hold on a minute.'

He fished a weighty tome from a hundred-guinea briefcase and riffled. He started to laugh. 'I thought she sounded familiar!'

'Is that it?' I smiled ruefully, 'One you had trouble with, I suppose?'

'That's her,' he said, drawing curvy feminine pictures in the air with manicured hands, 'With bells on. The same wee lady took us straight to the cleaners. Don't be accusing her of any debt she doesn't owe, for it ranks an expensive libel in this neck of the woods.'

I was grateful for the advice and looked courteously inquisitive as I freshened his coffee. He went on to explain.

'It started with one of those coincidences that happen once in a lifetime. Two successive tenants of that house had exactly the same name. The first one - and she's the one you're looking for, I bet my bottom dollar - disappeared over the border owing thousands all round her.'

Dear me. 'Tis only in Ireland you can do it. And bye-bye to commission on a few of those thousands.

'Treat the beauty who lives there now with kid gloves or she'll put a ring in your nose and lead you straight to the cleaners. She has a real smart lawyer backing her, that one. When our computer was new-fangled we mixed them up and lit a fire under the wrong one. The damages she took off us for defamation still give me nightmares. Thanks for the coffee.'

'Thanks for the advice. Hope we meet again, sometime.'

The next time I was in the office picking up accounts I got fingered by Sammy the One. 'That furniture account', he growled, 'did you put the frighteners on her?'

'If you will just sign this expenses chit,' I said, turning on the charm, 'I will, acting on information received, proceed in a southerly direction in pursuance of my enquiries.'

He had started to sign when he remembered that Ireland were due to play Wales at Lansdowne Road. Our Sammy didn't get where he is today by being taken for a sucker, as he assures us at every opportunity. I gave him the file, recommendations in triplicate.

'Write the damn thing off,' I said.

Letitia, you devious little siren, sitting there on my hat, crying your crocodile tears and conning me up, down and sideways into taking you to Court! Me? The best Collector in the business! Put a ring in my nose and take me to the cleaners, would you? I'll teach you a lesson, my lady!

They say the lady loves Milk Tray, so I went suitably armed. And I put her over my knee and whacked her bum with the box, not having a rolled-up account handy.

Her engagement-ring is exactly like Princess Diana's, and I hear my Bank Manager needed ice-water to bring him round. But I must point out- most reasonably, you'll agree - that it's a sound investment, apart from keeping you from noticing the one in my nose.

Love at First Sight

by

B Rafferty

It was her. At first I was not sure: after all it had been almost thirty years since I first saw her and now here she was, sitting in the garden of an old house in what used to be a good area of town. There was a red haired man with her, younger than me, but not by much. I kept the tinted windows of my car rolled up, I knew he could not see me watching them.

I studied her more closely. My God! how she had deteriorated over the years. I could still see what she had been like, all those years ago, but time had taken its toll of her. I looked at the red haired man and wondered if he had any responsibility for her sorry looks. He turned and looked at her indifferently, then spun on his heel and walked into the house leaving her alone in the garden. I thought about going over to her, but decided against it. After all I was waiting for my wife, and if I was not in the car she would play merry hell with me.

The years rolled away as memory took me back to the first time I saw her. It was a beautiful sunny day, I could feel the sun, warm on my back as I walked slowly along the shore road. The traffic was heavy and noisy and I felt as though I had swallowed most of the dust it was throwing up. My shirt was beginning to stick to my back when I saw a bar a little way ahead. There were a few tables outside and I decided a cold beer was just what I needed. A waiter appeared almost as I sat down, I ordered a beer, sat back and lit a cigarette. It was through the smoke that I then saw her, across the road, shaded by a potted palm. Do you believe in love at first sight? I didn't until that moment. The beer forgotten about, I stepped into the road, an old Bedford truck that had seen better days almost ran over me, the driver cursing me in a language that would have done credit to a sergeant major. I was across the road now, staring at her. She was the most beautiful thing I had ever seen. The sun shone on her giving her a lustrous sheen. In five years spent in the Merchant Navy as an engineer, most of them east of Suez, I had seen most of the wondrous sights of this world, but she took my breath away. I was staring at her so intently that I did not hear him approach, he just seemed to appear at my elbow, oily and sleek, rubbing his hands.

143

'You like her Sir? he said. I looked at her again, a classical beauty she stood out from all the others, hours must have been spent on her grooming.

'She looks all right,' I said, not wishing appear too eager, but I knew I just had to have her, whatever his price.

He turned to face her and put his hand out and stroked her. I immediately disliked him, it was almost as though he had defiled her. I had just been paid off from an old tramp steamer, plying its trade between Burma, Japan and Australia. I had my pockets full of tin, as the old hands would say, but I had no intention of just having her for a short time, I wanted to take her home with me. I could just see my old man's face when I showed up with her. I smiled to myself at the thought. And the neighbours! I would be the envy of every man in the street, not one of them could have had anything like her before.

My heart was pounding and my throat tightened as I said, 'I want to buy her outright for cash - how much?' I had six hundred pounds in my money-belt, the result of sweating it out in an engine room for eight months.

'For cash Sir?' he said, 'a special price for you, only five hundred pounds.' I wasn't going to argue; I wanted her, I pulled the almost new notes from my belt and counted out five hundred onto his sweaty palm, covering the heavy gold and diamond ring he wore. I wondered how many like her had sold to get that ring! I didn't care, she was mine, all mine. As he handed me a receipt he said, 'That's the second Mark 2 Jaguar I've sold this week.'

Visitors from the Stars

by

Ernie Larkin

I had just walked a few yards from the bus stop in the High Street when I realised I had left it on the bus. I turned quickly, waving my hands in panic, but the bus had just pulled away.

Before I got off the bus my attention had been drawn to a strange man sitting facing me. I thought it a bit odd considering it was freezing and the middle of Winter and here was this person with a vest and shorts on, even more weird was, he had sunglasses on.

I must get my camera back I said to myself, I must get the film developed, the only real proof anyone had, the only evidence that intelligent life existed, beings with minds far more superior than ours. I must have taken at least twelve pictures before I clumsily stood on a twig and frightened them.

Trying to collect my thoughts I noticed a taxi approaching, I quickly waved it down.

'Where to sir' the taxi driver said.

'To the bus station' I said in a panic sort of voice.

'But there are two stations in this town.'

'Great that's all I need,' shaking my head in disgust. Living on a farm miles from here this was my first visit to town.

The taxi driver spoke, 'I think I can help you, one station operates the out of town service whereas the other has a set route around the town.'

'It was a yellow bus,' I said quickly.

The driver turned on the meter 'no problem we'll be there in half an hour.' I lounged back in the seat and began to relive the experience that had happened the night before.

It was a cold crisp evening when I returned to my tent, I had been fishing down the river just about a quarter of a mile away, I put my gear down and started to collect some fire wood. Making a circle with some rocks I got a couple of sheets of old newspaper and placed some dry twigs on top, my hands were nearly numb as I fumbled to get a match out of the box, once lit the flame soon started to come alive as it fed viciously at the dry paper. The small twigs started to spark and crack as they caught fire, they seemed so noisy amid the

started to spark and crack as they caught fire, they seemed so noisy amid the stillness and quietness of the woods. It wasn't long before I had a nice fire going, I was starting to get some heat into me at last and had two trout cooking nicely, which I caught earlier. I lay back alongside the warm fire 'ah this is the life, living of natures land' I whispered to myself. I sat up and turned the fish over, looking up, the sky was so dark and clear and not a cloud in sight, the stars shone like diamonds on a sheet of black velvet, you could see the milky-way as its hazy path stretched from one end of the sky to the other.

I had just finished my fish, which I thoroughly enjoyed, and was about to enter my tent for the night when it happened. At a blink of an eye the whole area around me seemed to change from a winters night into a summers day, I could even see my shadow on the ground. Turning around and looking up at the same time, I was dazzled by the bright light above me, I put my hand above my eyes to cut out the glare, it was like starring at the sun, I had to turn away. Looking at the ground I noticed my shadow moving and the light getting less intense. I looked up again and to my amazement there was this object, this gi-gantic glowing disc moving slowly down the valley, its brightness lit up the immediate area directly below it. My heart was racing I could feel it pounding in my throat, a flying saucer, a UFO, I'd never seen anything like it. I watched as the craft started to pulsate, the light became dimmer as it came to rest in a clearing about one mile from me.

I ran to my tent, I must get my camera and get down there, I was shaking with both excitement and terror as I rustled through my bags. Having got the camera I started to run through the forest towards the clearing, the branches were hitting me on the head as I bored my way through the never ending wall of trees. I was breathing hard and tiring as I got within about two hundred yards from the craft, I stopped to catch my breath, I could see the clearing not far in front and the lights of the craft just beyond that. Calm down, settle yourself, I said to myself. I took the camera out of its case, I could hardly contain myself as I wound the film forward for my first shot.

Slowly I began to move forward to the edge of the clearing, the last few yards I got on my stomach and crawled just behind a dead tree. Making sure not to be seen, I looked over the tree and there in front of me was this huge dome shaped metallic object about the size of a house, I quickly focused my camera and began taking some photographs, I stopped suddenly when someth-ing caught my eye, slightly left from the craft I noticed three figures standing together, they seemed to be conferring with one another.

146

tureless, a small slit for a mouth, two dark patches for eyes, they were bald and had no facial hair. The best way to describe their face was like that of a human embryo in the early months of formation.

I was still clicking my camera as I tried to move in for a better look when a twig snapped under my foot, the three figures turned and stared at me, I quickly took another picture as they started to move behind the craft. I started to run towards the craft, but stopped as the huge object began to brighten, I had to move back the light was so intense and so was the heat.

I was just back behind the log when the spaceship started to hover above the ground, I couldn't understand it, there was no sound, no engine noise - ten feet, twenty feet and then with an unbelievable burst of speed it shot straight up into the night sky. I looked up but there was nothing, nothing but the stars and the darkness.

'Here we are Sir,'
'What' I snapped,
'We are at the bus station.'
'Oh sorry I was thinking of something else.'
'That's all right,' the taxi driver said smiling ' everyone seems to be thinking about other things these days.'
'How much do I owe you.'
The taxi driver looked at his meter, 'Six fifty will do.'
I gave him ten, 'keep the change.'
'Thanks a lot,' he said as he drove off.

I walked up to the bus station office window and knocked, the window opened, 'Yes what can I do for you,' a small elderly man said. I told him about leaving my camera on the bus, 'Oh yes that bus is in about ten minutes ago, in fact the driver is still in his seat doing some paperwork
'Excuse me.'
The bus driver pulled the window aside, 'can I help you.'
'Yes I got off in town and left my camera on your bus.'
The bus driver bent down, 'this must be your lucky day' he said as he dangled my camera out the window. 'Normally these things are never found, its a good job there are some honest people around, some weird guy dressed in summer clothes handed it to me.'
I spoke, 'was he wearing sunglasses?'
'Yes come to think of it he was, why do you know him?'

Not replying, I was thinking about the person sitting facing me on the bus as I opened up the back of the camera, the film was gone. Who was this mysterious man? Did he take the film from my camera? But most importantly where was he from. I lifted my head to the sky.

Rendezvous

by

Margaret Crawford

The journey had seemed endless. First the taxi from Belfast to Aldergrove. Then the long wait in the airport lounge - the plane was two hours late. The flight was routine, but Emma couldn't settle to read the magazine she had brought with her. From the air terminal at Heathrow, she had boarded the train. Now she sat in a second class compartment, gazing out of the window, seeing nothing, her mind slowed down to a point where she could only think about her eventual destination.

She was bitterly regretting the decision she had made to undertake this journey. But, being so close, there was no stopping now. If she did, she knew she would be back. Fatal attraction. She didn't want to be here, but here she was.

She tried to divert her thoughts to her family, back at home in Northern Ireland. John, her husband, had opted out of helping her to make this decision.

'If you want to, then do it!' he had said phlegmatically, and turned back to the football match on TV. Empathy was not his forte.

The children - well, teenagers are only interested in computers, loud music, and other teenagers of the opposite gender. She smiled faintly. They were good kids, but they couldn't possibly understand this riddle that she had spent most of her life pondering. And now that she had the key in her hand, she was afraid...

She had been eight years of age when she had first become aware of the factor that set her apart from the others. On the way home from school, dallying along a sunny country road, bickering with Jenny, a ten-year-old schoolmate, the first seed of doubt was spitefully sown -

'You're adopted!'

'Adopted? Of course not!' She said so in no uncertain terms. Jenny laughed scornfully. She came from a large family of older brothers and sisters and knew a lot of things an only child like Emma was too naive to dream of. She gave Emma a vigorous shove, then ran off up the summer road and turned a corner, out of sight.

Emma had been sent sprawling. She picked herself up ruefully and trailed homeward, absently aware of tar on her legs and on her white ankle-socks, from the melting patches on the road.

Her mother rubbed the tar off her legs with a dab of butter, then wiped it with a damp cloth. Whilst this was in process, Emma broached the subject uppermost in her thoughts.

'Mummy?'

'What is it? Hold still, Emma!'

'Jenny says I'm adopted. I'm not, am I?'

A brief silence. Then -

'Yes, Emma, you're adopted. Don't let Jenny upset you. She's just jealous.' Jealous? Jenny, who had her own mother, father, brothers and sisters, was jealous? She never figured that one out.

Things somehow weren't the same after that. She still loved the parents who had brought her up, but she felt different from the other children, an outsider with a guilty secret. Guilty, because, in the forties and fifties, being adopted carried a stigma.

As she grew older, she came to understand that stigma better. She realised that most adopted children were illegitimate, and that was something you had to be ashamed of. But why be ashamed? She hadn't asked to be born. Her real parents were the ones who should bear the guilt, not her.

Driven by a stubborn pride, she worked hard at school, passed exams, got a good job. And as she entered her twenties, she gradually relaxed and mellowed, coming to the conclusion that these things happen. What was done could not be undone.

John, whom she had met on a seaside holiday with some friends, was fun to be with. When their friendship developed into courtship, she had to confess her dreadful secret.

'What's so unusual about that?' was his response. He promptly named two people they both knew, who, he asserted, were also adopted.

'War babies,' he grinned, 'the Services left plenty of calling-cards here during the War.'

That was a crude way of putting it. But men tend to call a spade a spade. It was close to the mark. Her adoptive mother had told her what little she knew about her real parents. Her father had been in the Services - nothing else was known about him. She had marginally more information about her mother - her name and her home town.

After Emma and John were married, she had not been in any hurry to start a family. When she eventually discovered she was pregnant, her feelings were very mixed. She felt excited, yet apprehensive.

After Jonathan was born she was the victim of post-natal depression for several months. What caused it? Hormonal imbalance, or personality and background influences? Anyhow, it didn't happen when the other two were born. She loved being part of her family - settled, maternal.

Then she had started to wonder about the family she had never seen. What were they like? Did she resemble her father or her mother? How did her mother feel about it all? Did she ever think about the past? About her?

For many years there had been no means of finding out. Then, in England, for the first time, the law allowed you to trace your natural mother. But Northern Ireland had to wait for things to happen. Eventually the legislation was passed there too.

The Social Worker searched for several months before she traced Emma's mother to an address just outside London. She gave Emma the obvious warnings - her mother might not agree to a meeting - Emma would have to respect her feelings. Unexpectedly, anger and pain had welled up. After all this time, she was still vulnerable.

A few days' hiatus to rethink and settle her mind. Then she took the decision to continue.

Her mother was contacted. The reply came back; she had been married for many years. Her husband was unaware of her youthful indiscretion.

'Youthful indiscretion?' thought Emma, nettled, 'Is that what I am?' Her mother - Sarah - would agree to meet her, but as she had no plausible reason to travel to Northern Ireland, Emma must go to meet her in England.

So here she was, sitting on a train on its way to the small town where they were to meet at a pre-arranged rendezvous, a cafe called, unimaginatively, the 'Tea Shoppe.' They would recognise each other by their identical buttonholes, single pink rose-buds. Like a scene from an old B movie.

The train was beginning to slow down. This must be her stop. She suddenly wished John was with her. Rubbish, said her common sense, what good would he be? Standing up, she lifted down her travelling bag from the rack, and waited for the train to come to a standstill.

She was too early. The restaurant was almost deserted. Two men sat at a table near the door arguing about politics. An older woman in a navy, tailored suit was tucked away in a corner, reading a magazine; no flower in her buttonhole.

Emma decided on a cup of coffee and a scone and made her way to a table by the window. The bored waitress brought her order and slouched back to the cash register.

The coffee was luke-warm. She sipped it slowly. Her mouth remained determinedly dry; her stomach was churning. Eyes fixed on the door, she waited; her fingers strayed to the rose-bud in her lapel. Ten minutes dragged by. She glanced at her watch. The appointed time and arrived. Then another five minutes. Unbearable suspense. Perhaps Sarah had decided not to come.

The cafe door-bell jangled; she felt a sudden wave of overpowering panic, and plucked the rose-bud from the front of her jacket, crushing it in a jerky hand.

Two giggling schoolgirls appeared in the doorway, eliciting a scowl from the waitress. They demanded change for the telephone kiosk outside, and were grudgingly traded some silver for a pound coin.

Emma took a deep breath and opened her hand to survey the crumpled rose. As she did so, she became aware of a figure standing beside her.

Looking up, she saw a woman in her late sixties, in a navy, tailored suit, eyes brimming with tears, eyes the exact colour of her own. The woman raised her clenched hands from her sides and opened one of them to reveal a crushed pink rose-bud.

The riddle was at last about to be solved.

A Moment in Time

by

Vincent Dargan

The silence of the small dimly lit living room was broken only by the steady reassuring tick from the old clock standing proudly in the centre of the wooden mantelpiece. Close by the clock and placed at almost the same distance apart, stood two brass candlesticks, tarnished and veiled in a thin layer of dust. On a lower shelf and almost hidden from view, stood four generations of framed family photographs, arranged in order of their ascendency. They were visible only by the odd glimmer of light reflected from an occasional flame, escaping from underneath the well stocked coal fire. The room looked warm and inviting and very peaceful. As the few minutes to midnight slowly ticked away, the hands of the clock from inside the finger stained glass dome, took on the uncanny pose of a great orchestra leader. Guiding his musicians gently step by step, towards a dramatic climax in the musical score. On the wall opposite soft shadows cast by the flickering flames gracefully twisted and turned, like ballet dancers, through the patterns of flowers on the carelessly drawn window curtains.

The old man's chair creaked as he raised himself up onto his feet, and with his feeble hands firmly gripping the outer edges of the nearby furniture, he slowly shuffled around the room, making his way to the end of the hallway, towards the front door, to catch a breath of fresh night air. As he opened the door a discarded letter informing him of accommodation in a nearby nursing home fell from a cabinet in the hallway onto the floor. The passing autumn breeze had brought with it a light shower of rain and as he leaned against the outer frame of the doorway, he watched with interest how drops of rain running underneath the eves of a derelict house opposite gradually matured, as they swiftly encircled the dents in an overhanging pipe to make their escape. Cascading in perfect line formation, to fall to the ground, only to come to nothing and quickly vanish, as they hit the wet footpath below. Now he was thinking to himself how much the tiny drops of rain resembled his every passing year, and how so much of life had quickly passed him by, leaving him with only beautiful memories of how things used to be in the days of his youth.

153

By now the rain had eased, and his attention was then drawn by a familiar smell from the dust in the air as it settled on the damp road with a look of melancholy on his face, he stared deeply into the street. His tired eyes lingering for a moment at the empty spaces, where once rows of little terraced houses stood occupied by kind neighbours and friends. Now due to the demolition and redevelopment work in their area they had moved onto other parts of Belfast to make way for new roads and offices of an ever expanding modern city. As he looked about him he saw in the distance, the dramatic aurora of the many car headlights, lighting up the night sky creating moving silhouettes of ghostly shadows on the rubble all around him. At that moment fond memories of his youth flooded his head. Gradually his ears filled with the haunting lilt of soft singing voices that were familiar to him. As the sweet sound drew nearer and stronger it was now accompanied by a steady crescendo of marching feet. He saw the happy faces of many of his brave young friends pass him by as they headed off to war.

He silently recalled each one by name, and proudly stood to attention as he watched the vision of men from his regiment march row by row steadily out of sight. Their song 'It's a long way to Tipperary' now reduced to a quiet whisper as the throng of soldiers faded over the hill. Then, almost at once, another thought came to him of one beautiful day in August. The street where he lived was full of happy children jumping and running, through turning skipping ropes, singing their street songs about Dusty Bluebells and their Aunt Jane. Reeling with laughter, as others entwined themselves like wild ivy, with their swinging ropes around the old iron lamp-posts. Watched over by friendly neighbours sitting at their freshly painted doors as they chatted and enjoyed the summer sun. He recalled two young lovers making promises, as they walked together hand in hand. Then out of the hazy rays of the evening, he saw the young woman who was to become his bride walking towards him. As he reached out to embrace her, he was distracted by the sharp sound of a door slamming shut behind him. For a brief moment he turned his eyes away from the scene, and once again he was back to reality where he found himself standing in front of the boarded up remains of a place he once called home.

Just then he heard someone calling to him. It was the anxious warden from the nearby nursing home where he had wandered out of that day. She helped him into her car and as she prepared to drive away from the street she assured him it would take only a few more weeks for him to get used to his new home. As he turned to look back towards the house, he lowered his arm out of the open window of the car, and secretly dropped the keys of his old house, into the street grating, finally accepting that this was the close of a beautiful era in his full and happy life.

Trouble Afoot

by

Des Arnold

Probably the most morale sapping event in the social calender is the annual company dinner dance. The cigar-chomping board consider it more important to attend this rumour mongering shindig than your place of work. Earlier that day, had I not swerved to avoid an astrakhan-hatted motoring menace emerging from a side street, my weeded widow would still be expected to bravely turn up wearing a wan smile.

While my dearest was still undecided if that little floral number was due for an airing, I reached for my patent leather shoes. Both were for left feet! Recently my wife had discarded an old pair, and my vision became blurred as it dawned on me the bungle she had made. My flushed face reflected above her shoulder in the wardrobe mirror.

'You imprudent female,' I croaked, or something to that effect. 'I've got two left feet!'

'Don't I know it,' she replied, coolly.

Brown shoes or black wellies laughable, and failing to turn up at the firm's do unthinkable, I had visions of playing the ukulele in a subway while my wife washed clothes with flat stones on the canal bank. My true one appraised the situation.

'Squeeze your foot into one of them,' she instructed. 'The way you clodhop around the dance floor, nobody will notice the difference.'

The bizarre result saw both feet at five past one, the agony of a medieval iron boot, and the hopalong gait of Quasimodo.

'I don't think I'll make it,' I groaned.

'Of course you will. Just remember the area manager who failed to turn up. Y'know, the one who became a lollipop man.'

Hobbling painfully towards the garden gate, with a look of concern the taxi driver leapt from the car, and encircling me with a protective arm, eased me gently into the back seat.

'Would you care for a rug over your knees, sir?' he asked, kindly.

En route to the hotel, he kept emphasizing his admiration for the sorely afflicted who tried leading normal lives.

On arrival he carefully prized me out of the car and, promising to return, scowled at my loved one's retreating back.

'Never mind, sir,' he comforted, 'the day will come when all must answer to a higher authority.'

In the foyer the managing director and his wife greeted the guests. He had a cubed head and looked like Mussolini - so did she.

Each year she wore the same full length plain black dress with a single red rose peering coyly from an cavernous bosom.

'Did the taxi run over your foot?' she asked.

I laughed heartily. 'Just an itchy chilblain.'

Already husbands and wives had drifted into cliques at the bar, observing an unspoken caste system, and claims became bolder by the sip.

'I told Grimshaw what he could do with his bloody job! Went white he did, and...'

'My Derek has been offered the London branch on several occasions, but pollution would play havoc with Mother's sinuses, so...'

Following a forgetable meal, Mussolini called the diners to order by tinkling a glass with a spoon.

He smiled benignly at his flock. 'We've given solid food its chance, how about trying some liquid refreshment?'

The assembly roared with laughter, accompanied by much squirming in seats and slapping of thighs.

'He should be on the telly,' my neighbour choked.

'You could at least smile,' my wife hissed. 'Or have you another job lined up?'

A jolly cabaret followed with contributions from staff. An earnest young baritone from personnel, Adam's apple trembling, sang the glories of an open road with rain in his face, but an electric Hawaiian guitarist from wages proved most popular. In a fit of pique, the magician from maintenance timed to follow him pulled the plug at the onset of the third encore. Unplugged, the guitar had the resonance of a railway sleeper.

'Don't even consider doing your farmyard impressions,' my companion warned.

'Before we married you thought I was a scream.'

'I still do - but not for quacking like a duck.'

The three piece ensemble struck up a lively fox-trot, and by custom Musso and his wife made the first circuit of the floor. With exaggerated gliding steps and head swivelling like a puppet, he lacked only a number on his back.

157

My mate tittered. 'As usual you'll be expected to give her a twirl.'

'Are you mad?' I squeaked. 'The circulation in my mangled foot has slowed to a trickle.'

'It would stop altogether hanging onto a lollipop in a blizzard!'

Each year she feigned surprise. 'You rascal! Who would want to dance with a decrepit old lady like me?'

'I would,' I gushed, wishing that could be rephrased. I had taken only a few tortuous steps before emitting a groan.

'Are you unwell?'

'Just singing,' I chuckled.

By the second lap a casual observer would have assumed I was playing hop scotch.

Having reached the point of blubbering a confession and asking if there was a doctor in the house, the blood suddenly rushed back into my empty foot. The relief was short lived when I realized that due to unforeseen stress - the shoe was disintegrating.

The sole cracked like a slapstick in tempo with the bass drum before coming adrift; then came the cooling sensation of waltzing on my sock.

'That's better,' she cooed, as I spun her around. 'I think your style had become much too cramped.'

Twirling back to the disaster scene I tried kicking the abandoned sole under a table. Complete with nails, it resembled the lower jaw of a piranha!

'Who on earth lost that?' my partner asked.

'Dunno, but I doubt if anyone will report it missing.'

The music came to an abrupt halt and we found ourselves bathed in the spotlight. Having Musso's wife as a partner during a spot dance guarantees a prize, and the MC presented our gifts amid much applause and cheering. The only sour note being the solitary jeer from an assistant storekeeper who earlier in the day had been made redundant.

Ignoring the oath of sickness and in health, when my wife recovered from hysterics when I told her of my predicament, she opened my prize. It contained two pairs of tights!

Her eyes narrowed. 'Does this company know something about you I don't?'

Confronting the MC, he saw no reason to exchange prizes as no complaint had been received about my partner's bottle of after-shave.

An extrovert from home sales formed a conga chain, but the squealing revellers sheepishly dropped off one by one when he wove out into the car park and, with alternating kicks, pranced alone into the darkness.

My wife looked pleased. 'For a change you didn't take part in that silly spectacle.'

'You try doing the conga with one shoe and a spat!' I growled.

Musso strode centre stage, arm raised like a referee awarding a foul. 'All good things must come to an end,' he beamed, paternally, 'but I have excellent news concerning next year.'

'Goody, goody,' my mate muttered. 'It's being cancelled.'

'Our dynamic threesome, The Kentucky Stompers, to whom,' he waggled a roguish finger, 'you have tapped your toes all evening, will once again have you dancing a fandango with the lady of your choice.' He leaned back and peered sharply left and right into the wings. 'Or even your wife!'

The herd stamped and cheered to the point of delirium and my dining neighbour seemed ready for the last rites.

The caring taxi driver was perplexed, if not sarcastic. 'You've made a marvellous recovery, sir. When leaving home the only dance I thought you capable of was St Vitus.'

I slammed the front door behind me. 'In future the only thing you'll throw out without my say-so will be fish heads!'

She giggled. 'Supposing I said, I forgot to get rid of your old shoes - so you still have another odd pair in the wardrobe?'

Murder by Proxy

by

Paul Harvey Jackson

Every Saturday night we have a poker school; just the four of us, Bill Griffiths, Pete Duncan, Sam Jennings, and myself. We take it in turns to give the party, and to-night's my night - on my own home ground, you might say!

I glanced at my strap watch, it was seven o'clock. I fingered the still swollen scar on my cheek... any minute now the door bell would ring.

To-night's the night I take the biggest decision of my life. *I must decide if Sam Jennings and my wife are in love.*

If they are, Heaven help them. I know her, and I know him, I'll be able to tell all right! I reached the hall as the boys poured in...

'Hi fellas!' The poker table and drinks were in the lounge...

Glad slid in from the kitchen. She is a year my junior, but has worn well. She always managed to retain a sort of film star quality; good colouring, bright eyes, platinum hair - fantastic legs... We poured whisky, and settled down to play. I put Jennings opposite me. About my age, we'd worked together as mechanics in the same garage for some twenty years now. Not to be trusted, was Sam. Especially where women were concerned. Into the bargain he was always onto some fiddle or other. The latest one having to do with reclaimed television sets. His garage was stuffed with them... To protect this 'loot' he'd recently acquired a German police dog, one of those half-dog, half-wolf creatures - really vicious! He made sure of that; only fed it twice a week! I knew for a fact that the dog had turned on him already, and it was only by some deft warding off with a stick he kept for that purpose, that saved his life. One day; I thought....!

My mind ticked on relentlessly, computer-like, dwelling on an incident in the garage last month. At the time I'd put it down to an accident; but now I wasn't so sure. I'd been working on the engine of a Renault 1600, my head inches from the fan, when it happened, the engine turned over several times quickly, with the result that the fan blade gashed into my cheek bone. With blood pouring out of my cheek, I surfaced just in time to see Jennings slip, like greased lightning, out of the driver's seat. When tackled, he'd been apologetic - leaned in to borrow a screwdriver; brushed against the starter key... I was not over the

160

moon about his explanation, but because I couldn't think of any motive, gave him the benefit of the doubt, and let the matter drop. Twelve stitches it took to pull the wound in my cheek together. Years ago I remembered seeing Jennings kick a cat to death; so I knew that he was ruthless all right - but ruthless enough for....what?

All evening I watched him like a hawk watches a rabbit, and when the game folded about midnight, and the boys left, *I knew beyond a shadow of a doubt that Jennings and my wife were in love.*

In bed I said, 'Sam looked well to-night.'

Without batting an eyelid, Glad said, 'Suppose he did, I didn't really notice!'

The following Friday, I was doing a spot of overtime on a Volvo belonging to a friend of the boss. As usual the job was taking longer than I expected. Seven o'clock had come and gone, and I still had about an hour's work ahead of me. It was a particularly tricky rear-end operation, requiring much concentration. For the umpteenth time I squeezed myself under the waiting Volvo, perched without its wheels, like some great silver bird of prey, on two small hydraulic jacks, one at either side. The thought of using these small jacks for such a job infuriated me, and I cursed the large main jack for being out of order. A quick glance at my watch - eight thirty already. I fiddled determinedly in the region of the rear axle. What I did not know - and if I had, it would have brought great gouts of sweat rushing to my forehead - was that there was a fault in one of the jacks. Slowly, without a sound, it was allowing the mass of motor car to descend onto my unsuspecting body!

Half a minute later I felt slight pressure on my chest, and withdrawing my hand from the blackness of the rear axle, I quickly realised the danger. Aware that I had only seconds left in which to pull myself clear, and with ripples of apprehension playing a Bach Chorale up my spine, I propelled myself backward with all the force I could muster. Head free, and the rest of my body slithering clear, thoughts screamed through my brain... 'Twenty years in the garage business; never heard of a jack do this before...'

It was then that the worm of doubt struck... 'Could Jennings have planned this? Surely even he would draw the line at...murder?' Then I remembered he'd been using both the small jacks during the day! Suddenly my body stopped moving---my guts did a double somersault... Sweet Jesus... the hammer!

Sticking out of my overall pocket, and with the clearance between body and car now non-existant, the hammer had stuck; jammed fast under a rear chassis member. 'Help, dear God, please help me!' My agonised cries echoed emptily around the garage everyone had long since gone home. Like some panic-

161

stricken animal caught in a trap, and with the weight of the vehicle choking my life's breath out of me, I gave one final, hopeless heave - then lapsed into blackness.

Sometime later I awoke to find myself in the back of an ambulance, with the boss's quizzical grey eyes staring down at me.

'Where am I; what's happened?'

'It's okay Joe; just take it easy. A good job I forgot my keys, wasn't it? Everything's going to be all right - at least for you it is...poor old Sam's not been so lucky.'

'Why; what d'you mean?' I gulped.

'Sam was torn to pieces this evening by that damn dog of his. Apparently it jumped him when he opened the garage door...most peculiar, he must have had something on his mind. *You see, he'd forgotten his stick!'*

The Bed

by

William Kelly

Jim's majesty of red hair fell around his shoulders in primordial luxuriance. Drenched as it always was with gel it gave him the appearance of having just been fished out of the River Foyle. His large blue eyes dominated the show. They were always working overtime, looking here and there, shifting from long view to short view with habitual ease. This day they were livelier than usual. He was seated at a small table with his pal, Deeks. And Deeks who didn't know what his nickname meant nor anyone else for that matter was laughing himself paralytic.

'You've done it this time, mucker,' he managed to say. 'That's the weirdest thing I ever heard.'

So Jim told him the facts all over again.

He was on his own at the time, watching a pop-show on the box. His mother, with whom he lived, was in hospital. He had visited her that morning after signing on at the Unemployment Desk; and she was in good form cracking jokes with the other women in the ward. She would be out within the week, 'free as a bird', she'd said. Gallstones was the diagnosis and they were giving her a brand new medicine to put her right. They were 'spoiling her rotten', she'd laughed, and wasn't at all looking forward to getting out. She had a slight pain in her back, she added, but it was nothing to worry about. Weren't wee wanes dying of hunger all over the world? Jim left her and made his way to his sister Sharon's place. He stayed for a while to play with the three kids. Report delivered, he left quickly and walked homewards over the bridge. He was anxious to catch his favourite group on the telly. On the way he bought himself a bag of chips, slipped ten-pee to a wino who asked him for 'any odds', and dallied a while around the Guildhall Square to chat with his mates.

It was six-thirty when he returned to his empty house in the Bogside. The show had just begun when he heard the racket - a deafening clatter of bin-lids warning that an invasion of the army was imminent. They had gotten into the habit of making house-raids of late and everyone in the district was enraged, not only by the frequency of these raids but by the brutality of them. Property

163

was damaged as a matter of course and innocent people were dragged off. So, Jim abandoned his can of beer and his TV and went forth to investigate.

The people of the street were all at their front doors or scattered about in groups. A doom-laden expectancy had fused the air with menace. A huge barricade made up of anything combustible was being thrown together at the bottom of the street. Across from it, four or five pig-jeeps all wire-mesh and steel and belligerent as rhinos, stood ready to charge. In the meantime they were kept at bay by a shower of bricks that bounced off their green shells in a steady staccato. If the rampart could be got ready fast enough, and if it was formidable enough, it would block their way. The attack would lose its initiative and crawl back into the bush. Meanwhile, the bin-lids continued their cacophony. Kids were running around in a selfless frenzy their eyes crazy with excitement, and now several cars had lent their horns to the din. Jim could see the situation at a glance. It was the third raid this week and the sight did not surprise him in the least.

A neighbour came running over to him. He was shouting like a madman, waving his arms about.

'Get what you've got! An oul dresser, a chair, anything!'

That's when the idea came to him, he told Deeks. 'I swear to Jesus on me. . . Father's grave. I don't know what came over me.' He glanced at his friend. 'And it's not funny!' He sipped his pint and stared into the gloom. There weren't many in the pub on this dead Tuesday. Last night there had been total madness in his street. And now, here he was quietly sipping a beer. This was normal civilized behaviour but there was nothing normal anywhere. Normalcy, if it had ever existed, evaporated in 1969 when the 'troubles' started in earnest. In Jim's view the whole world was nuts. A suitable asylum would need to take on the dimensions of the moon.

That morning as usual Jim had visited his mother.

'You're not yourself, today, Jim', she had said, a concerned look in her green eyes. 'Are you eatin' all right, or gallivantin' all over the town? She paused, 'I hope you're not drinkin'. I mean it Jim. The judge said you would go behind bars next time.'

He had done his best to smile and shrug it off. His mother lay back and closed her eyes, a weariness suddenly coming over her. Of course, he couldn't tell her. That was out of the question.

So, he dandered over to the pub where he had arranged to meet Deeks. On the way he stopped at a furniture store: And that was where he found the solution to his problem. But, Deeks didn't seem too interested.

164

'Lemme get this straight,' said Deeks running a nervous hand over his thinning hair. 'You dragged your ma's bed out into the street and helped them to set it on fire?'

'I got carried away.'

'Now, you want to get her another bed?'

'Not just another bed, Deeks. An *orthopaedic* bed,' said Jim, wide-eyed.

'I don't care if it's got wings,' responded Deeks. 'You're talkin' five or six hundred quid for them yokes.'

'It would be a wee surprise for her, gettin' out of hospital, like.'

Deeks was confused. Why the bed? he asked himself. Why not a wardrobe or a table? But. . . 'the hoorin' bed - man's best friend?' And Jim didn't know why either. It was not as if Missus Burke had ever complained about her bed or held bitter feelings against it for whatever reason. He watched the lanky figure of his friend in jeans and bomber jacket amble up to the bar to get a couple more pints. He laughed to himself. Jim had done some daft things in his time but this one was way out on its own. Then he grew serious. Jim's solution to his problem was thinking from another dimension entirely. From the sublime to the ridiculous, as they say. Except this was from the too ridiculous for words to the too dangerous to be contemplated, in a two-pint state of mind.

Monday morning. The rain fell in a steady penance. Big dollops of it fell on the paving stones and on the flat roofs of the shops. The Post Office on the edge of the estate was packed with the elderly drawing their pensions when Jim and Deeks strode in wearing balaclavas. They waved imitation revolvers. Deeks ordered the two women behind the counter to hand over the contents of their tills. The audience muttered but were not unduly excited. This was the fifth robbery of the same Post Office in twice as many months. One old woman said to Jim:

'Do you want us to lie on the floor, son?'

To which he replied. 'Naw. Won't be a minute. Sorry about the masks and all but we don't wanna be recognized.'

'That's all right, son. It suits ye,' she observed in all seriousness. They took the money and put it in a black, army-surplus, holdall that they had brought with them. Then, they ran for two blocks and stashed the bag under the floorboards of a derelict house, to be collected later. It would be assumed that the Provisional IRA had done the job.

And so it was that a truck drew up at Missus Burke's house and a vast green bed with matching mattress was unloaded. Jim tipped the two men who carted it upstairs and put it together. When they had gone he got it ready, taking great

165

care with folds and pillows. He found a green eiderdown in the wardrobe, just the right colour. He would have preferred a pink bed but the man in the shop said they had only one such bed left and that was the one on display, and it was green: But, it he'd care to wait. . . Jim said not to bother, green was fine.

Later, he fetched Deeks to show him the end result. And then he took him to a pub for a few snifters. At least that was his intention but Deeks insisted on paying for the drink as he was quite 'embarrassed' with his share of the loot. They dropped into a Chinese restaurant on the way.

When Jim got home late that night he went upstairs to look at the bed and place on it the bunch of daffodils he had bought earlier. He lay on the firm, new mattress for a while to test it out. It felt good lying there in the amber lamplight that flooded into the little room. Across the street two drunks talked at one another by the lamppost. He adjusted the back-rest. His mother would have a clear view down into the street: She needed to watch who was coming and going. She had been like that ever since the soldiers burst into her home and beat up her husband. He had no doubt that she would rest easy now, although he would have difficulty in explaining to her where the bed came from. He would tell her that some charity or other had sent it over. He could hardly wait to see her face light up with delight.

Early next morning Jim awoke in his own room to find Sharon looking down at him. She had her own key and often let herself in when she wanted to hoover the house or generally look after things. She had never visited so early before and Jim was surprised. Then, he sensed that something was wrong. His sister sat on the edge of the bed:

'Jim. What'll we do?' And she burst into tears. 'It's me Ma. Jim I got the phone-call an hour ago. She's dead. . . Jim. She died suddenly during the night.'

Her brother's eyes stared at her, distant as a baby's, before filling up.

'She always said she would never die in his house,' consoled Sharon.

It seemed to Jim that, in that precise moment, he understood *everything*.

166

The Tramp

by

A Graham

Old Joe trudged wearily along the road, stepping this way and that to avoid the puddles which had formed from the last heavy shower of rain. With his tattered clothes and worn out shoes he looked a sorry sight as he headed in the direction of granny Moores cottage. Only a couple more bends in the road and he would have the village in sight and Grannie's cottage beckoning him for that welcome cup of tea and home made wheaten bread and jam.

Joe was a familiar sight in the village but unfortunately not a welcome one. Too often in the past folk would tell him to move on or after giving him disdainful looks, just ignore him. Only Granny Moore showed any Christian charity with her cups of tea. She would never allow him in the house but had no objection to him having his tea and a sit down in the garden shed.

Granny often chided him about his rough and tumble life 'you're not getting any younger' she'd say, 'its time you settled down somewhere,' but Joe loved the life he led. In summer he had no difficulty finding shelter and scraps of food. The winter proved more difficult but with people like granny around he had never gone hungry and anyhow, folk just took one look at him and shied away, so where on earth would he settle, as Granny put it.

As Joe neared the village there seemed to be more people about than was usual. He caught sight of PC Dodds and rather than risk abuse he dodged across the fields and approached Grannies house from the rear.

He found granny working away at her little garden, she greeted him pleasantly and bustled off to prepare a cup of tea for him. Joe settled himself in the shed and soon Granny arrived with the tea and homemade bread and jam.

Joe mentioned how crowded the village was 'Oh' said granny 'that's because some children have gone missing, they have not been seen since early this morning.' After some chat granny went off and left Joe to enjoy his tea, very soon he was nodding off with contentment.

It was late in the afternoon when Joe awoke and decided he would head onto his next port of call. As he and Granny did not stand on ceremony he headed off across the fields again to avoid the village.

167

As Joe passed along the backs of the houses he noticed some boxes and black bags at the rear of Bob Harper's yard. Bob ran the village grocery store and Joe was always sure to find something of use in Bob's rubbish.

He was having a good rummage when he heard a sound and he stood and listened, for if it were Bob he'd send him off with a flea in his ear. He had just resumed the search when he heard it again. He looked around him and the sound seemed to be coming from an old freezer some yards away. Joe approached the freezer, it looked dilapidated and badly rusted and did not look much good for anything but scrap. As he stood pondering, he heard it again, yes it was coming from the freezer. Joe attempted to push the lid up, it would not budge, it was quite heavy and took a lot of effort, with a last puff, up it came, Joe got the fright of his life, inside the freezer were two little boys. The bigger one was crying and his little hands were bleeding where he had been banging on the side of the freezer, another smaller boy was lying as if he were asleep. Joe gathered his wits about him and gently lifted the bigger boy out, he could barely stand. Joe was not a young man, how on earth was he going to manage the two boys, he looked around him in desperation.

A short time later it was a surprised crowd of people, including PC Dodds, who, at the shout of one of the bystanders, looked around to see this ragged tramp wheeling two children in a wheelbarrow. Like a swarm of bees they decended on Joe, everybody was talking at once, the children's mother crying and hugging the eldest boy. Someone ran for Dr Hickey and poor Joe was bombarded with accusations 'what are you doing with these children,' 'we might have known he'd have a hand in it' and so on until poor Joe's head was reeling.

It was hours later as Joe sat in the village police station that PC Dodds came in and said that the children were well, the little one had been unconscious but thanks to Joe's timely intervention, he would make a good recovery. The older boy had told how they had been playing in the old freezer and closed themselves in and had been there for hours until Joe came along.

Joe could scarcely belive it, suddenly he was a celebrity, within minutes of the word going around the villagers were decending on the station with clothes and food and telling Joe that from now on he could be a very welcome sight in their village, everyone wanted to show their gratitude. They realised it had been granny Moores kindness and hospitality which had brought Joe to the village from time to time and in coming today he had prevented a dreadful tragedy.

The Stranger

by

Brian Maguire

The saloon door burst open, as a low-set roughly dressed person pushing his
girl companion in front of him, entered down the single step and made their
way to the central table at which they sat down. He imperiously rapped the
glass top of the table, continuing the rat-tat until the white-aproned owner lifted
the counter flap and came over to take the order. His was a pint of cider, and
hers a large port. His rough gaudy clothing, cheap imitation jewellery, and his
incessant puffing of cheap cheroots, to the complete disregard of other people's
discomfort, betrayed his lack of taste and surplus of money. She was his junior
by several years, and was also flashily dressed, well endowed by nature, and
the plentiful application of paint and powder showed her type very clearly. The
saloon owner eyed them distastefully but took the order, and filling it up as
quickly as he could, returned to their table and placed the glasses on the beer
mats which liberally covered the table. He quickly sampled his pint, but did not
return the glass to the mat but instead put it on the glass table top adding its
ring to the many which were already there. The room was well supplied with
tables, each glass topped, ash trays many of them overflowing placed on each,
all of them advertising some kind of drink crisps etc, the floor was covered
with dark brown lino, which revealed many cigarette burns, showing that the
ash trays had not always been used!

The bar counter itself was very small being mainly taken up with several
charity collection boxes, beer mats, three well worn pump handles and a few
cardboard strutted ads for crisps. The walls were covered with further adverts
(This time for stout) a few mirrors and some 'pools' results leaflets. Along the
wall, as one entered the room was a padded bench, in front of which were two
tables again glass covered for easy cleaning and of course the inevitable ash
trays and beer mats. Sitting on this bench and so quiet that he was almost part
of the furniture was a stranger, his hair slightly greying at the temples revealed
his age. He was rather roughly dressed in a plain but warm looking overcoat.
He had an old felt hat tipped back, and the sweat-band of this hat gave evidence of several hot summers.

169

In front of the stranger was a pint tumbler containing a little stout, and several rings of froth adhering to the inside of the tumbler indicated that he had been there for some considerable time, and that he had taken an occasional drink but was evidently trying to make his pint 'last out'. There was only one other customer in the room, he was also sitting on the bench but was nearer to the door than the stranger. He ordered a beer which the owner delivered to the table in front of him. He came in just after the pair at the central table. Almost as soon as he spotted the stranger the semi-drunk growled across at him, 'Stop staring at my girl friend.'

She glanced quickly at him, plainly showing that she resented being referred to as 'my girl friend'.

The stranger quietly replied, 'I was not staring at anyone.'

The 'drunk' got up from his seat, awkwardly, almost spilling his drink in the process, his companion made an ineffectual attempt at restraining, him. He strode aggressively over to the stranger and with his livid face only a few inches from the stranger's he bellowed, 'Will you stop staring at her, I told you before.' He returned quickly to his seat, nodding triumphantly to his 'girl friend' by way of saying, 'I told him off didn't I?'

The stranger spoke quietly, 'I was not staring at her.'

Almost at once the tough got to his feet once more, and made for the stranger, he yelled, 'I told you before to stop it, and now you are at it again, maybe this will stop you' and he drove a massive fist into the unyielding face before him. Then he fell over sideways to the floor pulling his tumbler down and smashing it on the table. He pulled himself up putting one hand on the bench on which he had been seated, and the other on the table, cutting himself on the jagged pieces of glass. His hat rolled on its stiff brim towards the other customer seated further along the bench, and it soon came to rest at that person's feet. He then noticed that the stranger's walking stick which had been propped against the bench had also fallen to the floor. He handed the hat to the stranger who made no effort to take it, and then he noticed to his horror that the stick was white, he gently returned the hat to the stranger's hand, and placed the handle of the walking stick in his other hand. Helping the stranger to compose himself, he gently ushered him to the door of the room,

'One step up Sir,' he said, motioning the bar owner to throw out his untouched beer, he very gently guided the stranger along the corridor towards the street door.

'Two steps down Sir,' he said. The stranger descended to the pavement, shaking the blood from his sightless face, and waving his bloodstained stick from side to side feeling for obstacles.

The bar owner with a look of intense dislike on his face, advanced toward the person who had caused the trouble and said, 'Drink up and leave Sir, you have had enough and so have I.'

The bully got up, left the saloon, and reeled out of the Street door, followed by the girl, but the latter on reaching the pavement turned in the opposite direction, and walked off in the direction of the blind stranger.

A Train Journey with a Photograph

by

Gary Allen

We had never got on well. Near the end he hardly spoke, and I couldn't stand to be with him. A big, ignorant, useless man, nevertheless he outlived her by twenty years. When her mind eventually went and left her a fragile imbecile sitting immobile in her chair, holding an old tartan rug around herself smiling at nothing in the window, he shrugged and said he didn't recognise her, left her alone. The day they came to take her away, he refused to stay off work, saying what the hell use would he be? She didn't even bloody know him, sat all day staring at the God-damn telly. And when she died some months later, he said that was that, buried her quickly and never mentioned her again.

It had been almost dark when I had thankfully pulled the door closed behind me for the last time. The lights were on and the pavement was wet. Some children still played outside the terraced house, screaming and chasing each other towards the backs. The bunched top of the bin-liner kept slipping through my fingers - things I didn't even want - and I had to keep changing it from hand to hand as I hurried down to the station.

It is dark outside. Rain is smearing the window. The nearly empty carriage is reflected back. I want to smoke, but I forgot to buy cigarettes. The bin-liner is supported between my feet. I reach into the inside pocket of my jacket and take out the old photograph that I lifted from his bedside cabinet, wondered as I stared at it what it had meant to him?

A black and white photograph taken during the war. He is standing with a friend against a fishing-boat in Beirut. The sky stretched high above them. They are naked but for white-shorts. Why am I embarrassed by his body? Maybe I've never imagined him before, living as I have? Captured in that moment. Crew-cuts. White bodies. Time passing. Fragments. Things he said over the years coming back to me. Brought back by this picture, better than any memory I have kept of him.

Beirut. The blue of the sky falling down upon the white sands, down to the blue of the sea and the white-foamed waves that broke upon the biblical rocks. High, white clouds rolling past like the black smoke from the engine of the train to Derry, and the days that fell from a christian-calendar hanging on the

172

kitchen-wall of the small house down by the factory. And they put a rubber on Emanuel's nose as he slept, and every time he breathed out the rubber inflated like a balloon, as the back-yards flew pass the windows. And they stood like men dressed in their suits by the bar of the Royal and drank like men as the days fell to the ground like the betting-slips on the bookies floor. As they waltzed around the dance-halls, the Orange-halls, the Parochial-halls, smoking outside and drinking, exchanging blows, a hand on a leg if they were lucky. Time. Sending them off to war for a laugh. Tipping the orange-cart in Cairo. Oranges tumbling under the bright sun, rolling down the dusty back-streets. Arab curses, the flash of a blade. Run. Running with laughter and the sound of feet. Teaching the barman how to box while his friend rifled the till. Driving a truck along the desert road and running old Arabs out of the way with a swerve. All this from a man who couldn't find Cairo on a map. White Irish skin and thin legs standing in the burning sun, frying an egg on the side of a tank. Singing Kevin Barry on parade for a bet. The sergeant screaming into his face, 'you're a fucking Prod, Paddy!' Punching the sergeant in the mouth before being dragged off to the glass-house. Time passing in bread and water and the dropping of cards in the back-room of a bar in Cairo. Cheating? He probably was. And the Free French officer pulled a gun on him but he was too quick, hitting him across the dish with a bottle. Drinking cool beer in the insect buzzing heat, in the whirling of the fan-blades above his head as his mother was laid-out in the back-room of the little, dark house down by the factory. Time. Like the girl he waltzed through the streets of Belfast. Standing, red-haired, in her tartan-tammy as the tram pulled away and he caught her hand and led her to the marriage-bed and a child. Time. That took her away and became hands that turned him over on his back and probed his stomach. Time that took the sight from his eyes and choked him as he lay in darkness, that ran like fine sand through his fingers and made him realise that life had been an illusion after all. Meant nothing.

The train lounges into my station with a squeal, jerks to a stop and brings me back to myself. I put the photograph back in my pocket and stand, lift the bin-liner and walk up the carriage, open the stiff door and step down onto the platform. With an awkward gait I hurry down the ribbed incline, through the gates and across the station concourse.

It is cold and wet out on the pavement. I heave a sigh. He is gone. In my selfishness I had never tried to understand him. I certainly had no love for the man, nor is there any feelings of guilt - I am just overcome by my own loneliness. On the way by some closed shops, I stop and set the bin-liner among the bags

173

of rubbish left by the roadside, and - as an afterthought - I take the photograph from my pocket and set it on top, then hurry on.

The Decorator Comes to Call

by

Hugh Gallagher

If there's a china tea-set you don't need, if you're feeling depressed with the way your wallpaper is hung, send for Seamus Gillespie. A more decent man you'll never meet. Kind, considerate, good with the children, in many ways he is a saint. In our town he is famous, but for all the wrong reasons. You see Seamus is a painter and decorator, in his spare time.

The wife had been nagging me for weeks.

'The kitchen needs papering, and the hall and stairs, and the bathroom, and....'

I was at my wits end when who should I get chatting to in Molloys Bar, but big Seamus.

'I'm you man', he announced, as I related my troubles to the barman on Friday night.

'I'm thinking about tackling the job myself first, Seamus', I explained. His unshaven jaw sagged. I'd insulted him. I tried to recover my standing. After all it wouldn't be wise to cross a man of his size, I thought.

'Ach Seamus. Sure I was only jokin', man. How much?' I squirmed.

He moved closer like a tiger moving in for the kill.

'Now that would depend,' he announced.

'On what?' I asked.

'On how many rooms you want done.'

He flattened and rubbed his greasy black hair with the palms of his huge hands. The barman plonked another pint in front of him.

'Here Seamus, I'll get that,' I suggested, but he was having none of my tricks.

'I don't need nobody to buy me drinks,' he said huffily.

It was several minutes before he spoke again.

'I did this place ye know,' he said, sweeping his right hand around with a flourish.

'Is that a fact Seamus,' says I. I stared at the walls and the ceiling. There wasn't much to see. It looked alright, mind you, but I couldn't see whether or

175

not it matched properly because the lighting was so dull. The only section which stood out clearly was the yellow and red paper behind the bar.

'It looks grand Seamus', I said, bringing a broad grin to his solemn face. 'I'm just looking for the hall and the stairs and the kitchen done. The hall is split in two. Ye just have to do the top. Do you think you could manage that?'

'Dead easy,' he replied.

'How much?' I enquired.

'You get the paper and paint - strip the ould stuff - £40 the lot.'

Now I know a bargain when I see one. Quick as a flash I produced £20. 'I'll give you the rest when it's done', I explained.

As good as his word Seamus turned up dressed in a white bib and braces on Monday at four-thirty. I had stripped the old wallpaper at the weekend with the help of the children, Gary, Eddie, Mary and Cathy. The wife Mary helped as well, of course, between bouts of nagging. Just to try to make things right with her I even painted all the ceilings and skirting boards.

'Are you sure your man Gillespie will be alright?' was her constant enquiry. No matter what I said she continually quoted all the rumours she had heard.

'I heard he was a headbin. Did you not hear about him fallin' through Doherty's ceiling', she would say, 'People say he could just get up and chuck a job in the middle............ and oh aye - Mrs McLaughlin - know her down the road. Well, she swears he put her wallpaper on upside down.'

'And I suppose it's Gospel just because that ould gossip said so', I complained. 'Did you see the wallpaper yourself. Come on now. Where is your evidence? Answer me Mary', I demanded, but she kept silent.

Seamus was into his third roll of paper on the hall and stairs when I began to regret not tackling the job myself. He had knocked over a full bucket of paste onto the red carpet, and worse still he tried to blame me.

My son Gary ran around shouting, 'Daddy spilt the water, Daddy's spilt the water.'

When I thought about it, the paste did look like water. The wife refused point blank to clean it up. She called me into the sitting room when Seamus began papering around the wall lights.

'What's he at?' she shouted.

'Shush Mary. He'll hear you,' I whispered.

'I don't care. The big galoot. Look at the mess he's making.' He's choppin' the stuff to ribbons with them big scissors. He can't paper. Go out and stop him this minute.'

'Naw.'

176

'Right then I will,' she said.

'If you do. I'm going down to the pub. Right now. Ye canny treat people like this.'

'So that's it. You're sticking up for that eejit. It's him or me,' she declared.

'Or the pub,' I added sarcastically.

She quickly put on the childrens overcoats and slung on her own.

'Aw God Mary. Where are you going?' I enquired.

'My mothers.'

'I knew she'd materialize, sooner or later,' I said, 'Interfering busybody.'

'I'm away,' roared Mary, as she slammed the front door.

I could hear Gary asking her where they were going.

'A walk,' was all the reply he received.

'Listen Seamus. Do you think that paste is thick enough?' I asked when I had calmed down.

'Aye. That stuff would hold a boat sure,' he said.

I'll say one thing for Seamus. He was fast. At ten o'clock he had only one roll of paper to put up.

'Hi Seamus,' I said.

'What?' he replied.

'Would you mind if I went down to Molloy's for the last hour or so? You can leave the key in the door when you're finished.'

'No bother to me,' he answered, and carried on papering.

As I passed him some paste splashed on my coat, but it brushed off easily.

'See you later,' he shouted as I closed the door.

It was ten minutes to closing time when Seamus walked into Molloy's. I asked him if he'd have a pint, and to my surprise he accepted.

'It's finished,' he announced, hopping up onto a bar stool.

'Great stuff,' I replied. 'I'll have to go. Did the wife come back yet Seamus?'

'Naw. Not before I left,' he said.

I collected Mary and the children from her mothers in silence. Gary and Cathy were sleeping, so I got a taxi for the short journey home. My mother-in-law refused to speak to me. When the taxi arrived at our house Mary, carrying Gary in her arms, went to open the front door. I was busy paying the driver and helping the children out when she came running back and ordered them back into the car.

'What's wrong woman, for God's sake?' I asked.

'I'll be back when it's fixed. Take me to the address we've just come from, driver,' was all she said.

177

I stood scratching my head as the car drove off. When it was out of sight I rushed up the steps and gingerly pushed open the front door and switched on the light. What a sight greeted my eyes! Every second sheet of paper was lying on the floor and stairs or hanging off. After staring in disbelief at the mess for a while I made a mad rush at the walls and ripped it all off. Not that it required much effort. I threw it in the bin and went to bed disgusted. If I could have got hold of Seamus, there and then, I would have done him grave bodily harm.

'But then look at the size of the big eejit,' I thought, before I went to sleep.

On Tuesday morning, bright and early, I went out and bought eight rolls of the same wallpaper and did the job myself. I phoned my workplace and told them I was sick. In a way, it was the truth. Later, in the evening, Mary returned with the children. After seeing my efforts, I was forgiven.

At about quarter to ten I answered a knock at the door. The wife was taking a bath and the children were asleep. It was Seamus in his working gear. He pushed past me.

'Great job, eh!' he declared, feeling the paper, 'Not a bubble in sight. Sorry I'm late.' He lifted the plastic bucket and went to the kitchen sink to mix paste.

'Naw Seamus............. er............. Here hang on Seamus,' I stammered. I put my hand in my pocket. He turned off the cold water tap. 'Here's your money,' I said handing him a tenner. 'It's all I have left. The wife wants me to tile the kitchen instead now. Know the kind of these women!'

'I'll do that for ye sure,' he offered.

'Naw. I mean I've...... I've already asked somebody - Jim Devine,' I lied.

'Well, d'ye see you. You're wan ungrateful lousy sod,' shouted Seamus before marching out of the house.

'Who was that there at the front door love?' asked Mary, emerging from the bathroom in her pink dressing gown.

'Naw. Nobody love. It was nobody. Nothin' to worry about. Just........ just an insurance man. I didn't buy anythin,' I stammered, breathing a sigh of relief as she appeared to believe me.

She changed the subject. 'When are you going to do that kitchen?' she asked.

'Maybe tomorrow', I replied. 'Or next week. Do you want me to get big Seamus?'

A china teacup sailed past my right ear and smashed against the fire-place.

I swept up the pieces and said no more.

The Atheist

by

Jack Scoltock

'I'm very sorry, Mrs McGartan, but your husband has just passed away.......'

Paul McGartan stared down at the scene before him. He could see himself lying in the hospital bed and the doctor telling his wife that he was dead. His mind reeled as he tried to establish where he was looking from. It seemed to him that the was somewhere in the corner of the ceiling.

'What do ye mean, I've just passed away?' Paul yelled. 'I'm here...... here. Can't ye see me?'

He struggled to try and get closer to his wife and the doctor but then he saw them begin to fade away. Suddenly, he was being whisked along a dark tunnel. Away ahead he could see a bright dot growing larger as he drew nearer. Now he was passing through a bright shimmering light and as he passed through it he felt filled with a warm, peaceful glow. Suddenly, with a low whoosh, he stopped.

'Could you please join the queue, sir.'

'Eh?'

Paul gasped in astonishment at the golden haired being with shoulder to heel white wings.

'Could you please join the queue for judgement, sir.' The winged being pointed behind him. 'It won't take long, sir.'

Turning in the direction the being indicated Paul saw that there was a queue of people. Swinging back to ask why they were queuing, his mouth fell open as he saw the Angel fly off.

In a daze he stumbled to the back of the queue. Still dazed he tapped the shoulder of the man in front of him and asked, 'Where are you from?'

With a frown the man turned and answered, 'Belfast. You?'

'Derry. Tell us mucker, what happened to ye? How did ye snuff it?'

'Snuff it?' the man said puzzled.

'Aye, snuff it. Ye are dead, aren't ye? We both are, aren't we?'

'Oh aye, we're dead alright,' the man said smiling. 'Me, I was shat.'

'Shat? What's that?'

179

The man stared at him for a second then said, 'Shat......... with a bullet........I was shat.'

'Aw, ye were shot. Why didn't ye say so? What happened?'

'Dunno. I was coming out of church today and they shat me.'

'Church? Ye believe in God then, do ye?'

'Aye, of course I do.......... don't you?'

'Naw I don't,' Paul snapped angrily at the same time thinking, what am I doing here anyway?

The man stared at him, then said, 'Well you'd better start believing in him right and quick, you're about to be judged you know.' Turning he nodded to the head of the queue and then Paul saw them.

An old man; a very old man with a pink wrinkled face and a long wispy white beard that seemed to melt into his fleecy white robe. In his hands he held a thick golden book. Standing beside him was a woman; a beautiful golden haired woman. Her long hair fell to her slim waist. She wore a blue garment that stretched to her porcelain like feet. On each foot was a perfect red rose, and around her waist hung a gold linked belt with a tiny red cross buckle. She was the most beautiful creature Paul had ever seen.

Two minutes later, Paul and the man in front of him were at the head of the queue. He watched as the old man closed the book with a loud snap and the Belfast man was led away, crying. He looked back at Paul for a moment then an Angel tugged at his arm and they disappeared into the clouds.

Now the old man addressed Paul.

'Welcome, friend Paul. My name is Peter. You are welcome. You are about to enter Heaven.'

Paul gulped as he stared at Peter. He had the golden book open and a feathered quill suddenly appeared in his hand. With a quick stroke of the pen he then snapped the book shut and smiling he addressed Paul again.

'A few tiny errors on the way, but you made it. Welcome again to Heaven friend Paul.'

At last Paul found he could speak. 'Heaven!' He gasped. But how can I be in Heaven? I'm an atheist. Don't ye know that? A friggin' atheist. I don't believe in Heaven......... or God fer that matter. So what's all this about, mucker?'

Peter smiled at his companion.

'Oh we know you didn't believe. That is why you are here. You see you couldn't commit any sins against God because you didn't believe.'

Behind Peter and his beautiful companion Paul could see Angels playing harps and flying in and out of the fluffy clouds. Through a gap in the clouds he could see a shimmering path that wound away to a lovely valley of quilted greens and silver rivers.

'Is. . . is that Heaven?' he stammered.

'Yes. Come, let us take you there.'

Reaching out Peter took Paul's arm but with an angry grunt Paul pulled away from him.

'Wait! Wait just a friggin' minute mucker. I told ye I don't believe in Heaven. I don't want to go down there. Look, there has to be a mistake. Are ye sure ye have the right person. I mean, I'm an atheist. A friggin' atheist.'

Turning to the woman Peter smiled, then turning back to Paul he said, 'There was only one atheist called Paul McGartan in Derry. You are he. There is no mistake. Come, you belong in Heaven.'

Paul grew angrier, 'Oh I do, do I. Well what about that poor sod from Belfast? What about him? He belongs in Heaven. He was shot ye know. What about him, eh?'

Peter's old eyes grew sad as he said softly, 'He will be welcome in Heaven after a time. First he has to be cleansed of some errors. But you friend, Paul McGartan, you can go straight on in.'

'Naw. . . naw,' Paul said loudly growing even angrier. 'I don't want to.'

Frowning Peter turned again to his companion who smiled but said nothing. Her blue eyes flitted over Paul's angry face. Then looking at Paul, Peter said, 'You have to come into Heaven. You have to. You can't want to got to the other place? Not with him, surely? Not with Lucifer? You must come into Heaven. . . You belong there.'

Paul glared defiantly at old Peter. Then the golden haired woman suddenly reached out and took his hand. The warmth and gentleness of her touch surged through him and he immediately felt at ease. She looked into his eyes and spoke, her voice singing and soft.

'Come. . . come with me, Paul. I will take you down to the golden gates. Come.'

Paul hesitated.

'Come,' the woman repeated and he allowed her to lead him through the clouds past hordes of singing Angels and onto the shimmering path that led to the beautiful valley. 'You will like it there, Paul. You will be able to have anything you desire.'

'Anything?' Paul whispered, staring in awe at the scenes all around him.

'Yes,' the golden haired woman said, smiling.

Soon they came to the open golden gates and through them in the light mist Paul could hear the loveliest singing. Suddenly, he felt panicky and with a great effort he pulled his hand from hers. The woman smiled at him.

'Don't be afraid Paul. You have nothing to be afraid of.'

'Ach, I'm not afraid,' Paul said quietly. 'It's just. . . It's just. . . well, look I find it hard to believe. I mean, I've been an atheist all my life. I've never believed in anything. I've never harmed anyone right enough and I don't think I've committed any big sins, but still I find it all hard to believe that I'm about to go through the gates of Heaven.'

'Yes, you are.'

Paul stared at her for a few seconds, then asked, 'Look, tell me. When I'm in there will I see him?'

'Him?'

'Aye, him. . . God. Will I be able to see God?'

'Of course,' the woman smiled.

'Well tell me, what does he look like?'

Smiling the woman took his hand again and led him through the gates.

'I am God,' she whispered, and the heavenly singing surrounded him as he passed into eternity.

The Christmas Pinta

by

Irene Nobbs

William woke up on a cold grey midwinters morning with a sinking feeling in the pit of his stomach.

He lay, warm in his narrow bed trying to remember what it was in this particular day that was more depressing than usual. When nothing came to mind, he reached out a gnarled hand and switched on the radio on the bedside table.

The strains of 'O Come All Ye Faithful' filled the room, and instantly he was reminded of the reason for his depression. It was Christmas day. A day for friends and family, good will and cheer. Certainly not a day for sitting, old and alone, in a gloomy suburban bedsitter. He switched off the offending carol, with the cruel reminder of childhood Christmases long ago, and sitting on the edge of the bed, pushed his feet into his battered carpet slippers. Belting his ancient dressing-gown over his flannelette pyjamas, he shuffled down the corridor to the communal bathroom. He was relieved to find it unoccupied, until he remembered that it was probably meant that all the other tenants had gone else where for Christmas. As far as he knew he was the sole inhabitant of the four-storey terrace house. It was an eerie feeling to be all alone in a big house.

Back in his room, he switched on the electric kettle and made tea and a slice of bread and marmalade. He carried his plate and cup over to the electric fire and switched on one bar to dispel the chill.

Electricity was an awful price, but at eighty-seven he knew he had to keep warm. If he didn't he might end up with hypothermia and that would be the end of him.

He considered getting back into bed, but decided against it. If he did he would be tempted to spend the day there and maybe the next, and before he knew it his legs would seize up and he would find himself bedridden - depending on other people for everything. Whatever happened he had to keep going.

He finished his tea but he still felt hungry. He thought of boiling himself an egg, just because it was Christmas, but decided not to. It would make it seem like a special day, and there was nothing special about it. It was a day like any other day, only worse - much worse. Couldn't even go to church. The church was half a mile away, and he couldn't walk that far.

There wasn't even the meals on wheels lady, Mrs Brown to look forward to. Mrs Brown with her determined cheerfulness and her awful habit of bouncing in with a hearty, 'Well, and how are we today?'

Which never failed to infuriate William. He detested Mrs Brown, but at least she was a diversion. A change in the dreamy pattern of the hours between getting up and going to bed again. Meal's on wheels ladies didn't come on Christmas day. The one day when they might be appreciated most. As he munched his way through his second slice of toast, William pondered gloomily on the unfairness of a fate which decreed that some people should be alone and friendless whilst others seemed to be loaded down with children and grandchildren.

He reckoned he would have made a good father, given the chance, but he never had a chance - he was the plain one of a handsome family. True, he had brains, but in his younger day, brains were not a much sought after commodity in a man. One by one the rest of his family had married, leaving him to look after ageing and ailing parents, but instead he found himself at the age of sixty five alone and unmarried, with his talents shrivelled through lack of use.

The only woman who had wanted to marry him had been a friend of his mothers. He had liked her but the thought of marrying someone thirty years his senior did not appeal. Years later he had regretted his decision. He might have given her a child - someone of his own to love, who would have loved him in return, someone who might of saved him from a lonely old age. He heaved himself up with a sigh and shuffled over to the kitchenette, where he poured himself another cup of tea.

When he poured it he suddenly remembered the milk was finished. He'd used the last drop for his previous cup. He clicked his tongue in irritation, there should be a pint waiting for him on the doorstep - as long as the milkman hadn't taken Christmas off as well. But it was a long way to the front door. His bottle of milk was on its usual spot on the front door step. He heaved a sigh of relief when he saw it. Thank heaven for the milkman! He had never let him down yet. He at least hadn't forsaken his customers just because it was Christmas. Stooping he picked up the bottle and carried it inside. As he was about to mount the stairs again, the door on his right opened abruptly, making him jump. The new tenant emerged into the hall. She had been there for about two months, but William had only seen her twice but had never spoken to her. He didn't like the look of her. She was a small dumpy woman with a wrinkled face covered with a thick layer of powder and clothes which were completely unsuitable for her age or her shape. Today she dressed in an emerald green trouser suit, which made her look like a garden gnome! William reckoned she was well into her seventies - maybe even in her eighties, not much younger than himself anyway.

He nodded curtly and started back up the stairs. Behind him he heard the front door open and close, then a voice behind him said loudly and clearly, 'That's mine!'

William froze for an instant, his heart racing. Surely the woman couldn't be talking to him, no, of course she wasn't - the thing was impossible. She must of been speaking to someone in her room - some visitor. Recovering himself, he plodded on up the stairs. He had only taken a step when the voice came again, more sharply. 'Hey! are you deaf? that's mine I tell you.'

William stopped again and turned round very slowly. The woman was standing below looking up at him, her stout green legs apart and her hands on her hips. Her chin stuck out aggressively. 'You've taken my milk,' she said indignantly. William could hardly believe his ears. 'I beg your pardon,' he said with as much icy dignity as he could muster.

'You've taken my milk,' the woman repeated.

William stared at her, open-mouthed in amazement and anger. 'I most certainly have not,' he said at last.

The woman bustled, 'I left a note out for the milkman last night.'

'I don't care what you did,' William retorted, 'he leaves me a pint every second day, and there was none yesterday so this ones mine.'

'There you are, you've admitted it. You didn't actually ask him,' she said.

'Of course I didn't, I don't have to. He should know my order by now, I've been here for twenty years and I've always found him completely reliable.'

The woman looked sulky. 'Well, either he made a mistake or you did, but that one's mine anyway.'

'It certainly is not.'

'Yes it is.'

'No it isn't.' They glared at one another. William realised that he had the advantage. He had the bottle in his hand. If the woman had been decent about it, he might have given her some - but as it was...

'Anyway you're out of luck,' he said nastily, 'I got it first, so there.' Turning he continued his journey up the stairs. The woman's voice followed him. 'Mean old twister.'

William reached the safety of his own room and went in banging the door furiously behind him. He flopped down in the chair by the fire, aware that his heart was pumping like a sledgehammer. What a dreadful, vulgar woman. He'd complain to the landlord about her next time he saw him. Maybe he would evict her. After all he was one of his oldest tenants. He didn't see how he could go on sharing a house with someone like that.

The morning and afternoon crawled by with agonising slowness. When his anger cooled, William washed and dressed himself in his everyday trousers and jumper and went through the motions of cleaning his room, though it had been cleaned thoroughly the day before. He straightened the two Christmas cards on the mantelpiece - one from a dutiful nephew in Canada, and the other from his only surviving brother in Scotland. There was no other reminders of Christmas, except when he turned on the radio, so determinedly he kept it off. It was lonely without it. He had no television, and normally he found the radio good company, but not at Christmas. The house was as silent as the grave.

After his meagre lunch he put on his glasses and tried to read a book. It was a good book, one he had been saving up specially for Christmas day, but he found he couldn't get into it. He read the first page over several times, and even then it hadn't sunk in. He knew the reason only too well. It was that wretched woman downstairs. Why couldn't he just forget her? She didn't deserve to be thought about, he tried to blot her out of his mind, but the more he did the more he thought about her. Maybe she couldn't drink black tea or coffee. He, William had left her tea-less and coffee-less on Christmas day. It wasn't a very neighbourly act, whatever way you looked at it.

As the grey December dusk was beginning to decend, he rooted out a small glass jug, rinsed it, and poured half the milk into it. Then, carrying the jug, he set off on the long journey back downstairs. He had just reached the hall door when the woman's front door opened and she emerged. Their eyes met, they stared at one another for several seconds - then William broke the silence.

'I'm sorry,' he said stiffly. 'That was unpardonably rude of me. I've come to apologise and to give you this.' He held out the jug of milk awkwardly. The woman looked at it and back at William. Her face was grim. For a moment William thought she was going to knock it out of his hand, maybe even hit him. Then suddenly the woman smiled and her face was transformed. It was a warm, lovely smile, as if a light had been switched on inside her.

'That's funny,' she said 'I was just going upstairs to apologise to you. Must be telepathy.' Turning she held open the door of her room. 'Come in' she said 'no point in standing out here in the cold.'

The room was warm and cluttered and smelt of talcum powder. Half a dozen Christmas cards adorned the mantelpiece, and a big vase of holly and ivy sat on top of the television. An open fire burned in the grate. The effect William found quite cosy. The woman took the jug of milk from him and motioned him to a seat by the fire. Then she went over to the kitchenette and produced a bottle of sherry from the cupboard.

'My son brought me this the other day,' she said. 'But I've nobody to share it with, and I don't like drinking alone. It's lonely all by yourself on Christmas Day.'

'I know,' William said feelingly, as he held out his chilled hands to the fire.

'Have you any family?' the woman asked.

William shook his head, 'No, I never married.'

The woman produced two cut-glass sherry glasses and filled them. She handed one to William. 'Maybe it's better that way,' she said.

William swallowed. 'I don't know what you mean,' he said. 'I don't see how it could be.'

The woman shrugged. 'Well, what you've never had, you never miss. I've got two grandchildren, but I'm still alone at Christmas.' She tried to smile, but the smile wobbled and went crooked at the corners. Tears came into her eyes and overflowed down her wrinkled cheeks, making tracks through the pink powder. 'Nobody wants to spend Christmas with a lonely old woman like me,' as she sniffed and groped for her handkerchief.

'Except perhaps a lonely old man like me,' William suggested. He raised his glass, 'here's to a Happy Christmas,' he said.

The woman lifted her glass and clinked it against William's. 'Let's kill the bottle,' she said recklessly.

Five hours and dead-bottle of sherry later. William climbed the stairs a trifle unsteadily to his own room. He had found out that his new neighbours name was Dora - that she was a widow of eighty three - that her daughter lived in Australia and she didn't get on with her sons wife - that she could make delicious apple tarts - that she too detested Mrs Brown and that she'd always wanted to try a hand at painting pictures. They had made tentative plans to enrol for art classes at the school round the corner in the new year.

William thought he might even join a creative writing class, Dora had an old typewriter which she'd promised to lend him if he ever wrote anything worth selling. She also told him that if he ever wanted to watch anything on television, like the special programmes for New Years Eve, he had only to ask.

William filled his hot water bottle and climbed into bed, his mind buzzing with ideas. He switched on the radio, then he lay back, and began to work out in his mind, the plot of his first short story.

Down below in a dark hollow in the ground beside the steps leading up to the front door, a straggly black cat with half a tail missing finished off the remains

of the bottle of milk which he had knocked of the door-step earlier. He took
great care to avoid the splinters.